Millport Memories

Or how I learned that thirty-three visitors, myself included, with little else in common, could see Millport and the Isle of Cumbrae in a similar light and maintain a love of all its eccentricities.

I A peaceful harbour flanked by the Royal George Hotel.

Millport Memories

by

Edwin Deas

Novels by the Author:

Crises on The Cumbraes

Six at Cambridge?

Calum's Shorts

Murder on The Waverley

Keep in Touch with the Author:

edwindeas1@gmail,com

www.facebook.com/edwindeasbooks

www.linkedin.com/in/edwindeas

Millport Memories

Edwin Deas

Cover design by Bronwyn Jenkins-Deas

Editing by Bronwyn Jenkins-Deas and Dr Helen Ralston French

First printing in 2022

Published by TannerWorks in association with Kindle Direct Publishing (KDP)

ISBN 9798835483303

This book is dedicated to the thirty-two intrepid volunteers, who selflessly shared their lifetime memories for my benefit, and contributed to many laughs along the way.

In addition, it is dedicated to my wife, Bronwyn, as always.

II A busy Kames Bay at low tide.

Contents

Chapter 1.

Forethoughts

III West Bay taken from Cosy Corner.

I must have been two or three years old when my parents took the family for the annual fortnight's holiday all the way to that exotic island on the other side of the country. Of course, my brother, Ian, seven years older, had the advantage of already being a seasoned visitor because that was where my family always headed. But from 1952 or 53, I first experienced the joy of life on an island for myself, where everything was different from home in Edinburgh, or even from the mainland. The country had been crossed and then the train exchanged in favour of a paddle steamer for a veritable sea voyage to Millport. Just getting there was an unforgettable adventure and once installed, fourteen days of unbridled joy and pleasure were inevitably to be had. No period of fourteen days ever made a greater impact on my life but then again, no fourteen days ever passed so quickly and triggered the excitement of looking forward to the next holiday the following year.

So, a lifetime of memories was developed, though a lifetime that never seemed to stay the same for very long; from childhood without a care in the world; to the rebellious teenage years; to the loss of a father who only ever seemed totally relaxed in Millport; from marriage and children of my own and finding ways to maintain the holiday tradition where I was now the leader but fully intended to simply carry on my childhood habits; and to later in life when one has the desire to look back on life as much as looking forward and where the decision was made to spend longer and more frequent periods there. Millport and the Isle of Cumbrae was always there for me. It was the one constant in an ever-changing lifetime.

That did not mean that I did not travel to other places. I have been very fortunate to have visited many exotic places throughout the world and to have lived and worked in three very different locations--- Scotland, Canada and USA. And yet, the Island has always drawn me back like some powerful magnet. Just when I might feel that things were getting on top of me in a stressful demanding career, relief was always around the corner, sometimes carefully planned over a long period of time and sometimes on the spur of the moment, when I was able to step on to that ferry, the exotic steamer of days gone by or the somewhat humble craft of recent years, and all my worries would disappear. I was heading back to my spiritual home---that place where only good things happened and where the more it changed over time, the more it stayed the same!

From my very first visits, all the way through to my most recent, I always considered Millport to be a well-kept secret. Not many of my friends had ever heard of it, far less visited it. Even the Scottish friends that I had maintained after leaving the country for Canada in 1982, were only vaguely familiar with it. After my father passed away in the mid-60s, my mother chose not to set foot on the Island ever again. I never really understood that one. And even worse, my brother, around about the same time when he was moving into marriage and having children of his own, made a similar decision. That one baffled me too. Yet still I continued to visit as often as I could and my own children, who had initially fallen in love with the place, eventually found the distance from Canada and the alternative things on offer there to be sufficient justification for staying home. Eventually, there was just me and a new wife to maintain the tradition. Bronwyn was a Canadian native and had never heard of the Island, far less visited it!

In all that time, I maintained the belief that precious few people were aware of Millport and only I alone was blessed with experiencing that sense of euphoria every time I set foot in the place. Fewer and fewer people seemed to be visiting for two weeks or more, or even coming on a day trip as the new millennium rolled around. The place seemed to be slowly dying a mysterious death. Yet, it never caused my pleasure to diminish, and I was greatly surprised when Bronwyn took to it like the proverbial duck to water. She was an even greater world traveller than I, but somehow the quaint little Victorian town and pastoral island captured her imagination.

Our more frequents visits came about because we often had business in the UK or elsewhere in Europe. We adopted the mantra of "Why don't we pop over to Millport as we are in the neighbourhood?" In reality, we were often nowhere near the place, but we frequently managed a trip, even if it was for only a couple of days. And more than once it was in the dark, Baltic days of winter. That is proof of a true obsession! These visits seemed to unearth people from all over Scotland, and far beyond who were doing exactly the same as we were. In any couple, there was inevitably one person who had an almost identical DNA to me. They had been brought to the Island as a child almost every year, then they had married and had a family which had been let in on the secret and brought frequently. Now their children were grown up and it was back to the couple on their own continuing to make the pilgrimage. And maybe even to put down some semi-permanent roots in their spiritual home. I was beginning to realize that

3

I was not unique. I had probably just not taken the trouble to stop to talk to people in Millport enough. I was too intent on enjoying myself.

What really confirmed that my secret place was actually well-known by an incredible number of people was the advent of the internet. Gradually, there was communication around the world on all sorts of topics of common interest and I learned that many of them had to do with an island…my Island! People just loved to reminisce about their summer holidays "Doon the Watter" as children, and how their lifelong interest had caused so many to start visiting again. Those people might live in Largs, so no big deal to hop on the ferry when they felt the urge, but a great many were from places nowhere near Largs, in fact scattered all around the world, and they thought nothing of hopping over too. And even those who could not make the trips, could enjoy the next best thing---just talking about the Island and sharing tales. The tales emerged from what felt like a simpler time when only good things happened. I don't know if there was an unwritten rule on those websites that precluded negativity or else it was just the magic of the recollections that ensured that only good things happened and were longingly reported and commented on.

Upon retirement, I realized I had no hobbies, so I took up the writing of fiction. Once I had published four novels, all with healthy Cumbraean content and Millportonian plots, I began to connect up my literary interest with my newfound awareness on the worldwide interest in the Island generated through the internet. The one drawback of the latter is that the content is fleeting. You read something of interest; the next day, there might be some shared comments; but pretty soon the focus has moved on to something else, and all those first interesting comments have disappeared. And information is jolly difficult to retrieve later on. Once a week has passed by, it feels like it has gone forever. I determined that the information contained in a book is much more lasting; in fact, it can be everlasting if one has enough room on the bookshelf. I considered the compilation of my own memories but quickly decided that would be one-dimensional and perhaps only of interest to a couple of readers…Bronwyn and me! Therefore, it came to me that the book should contain the memories of as many people as I could handle in order that they could be compared and contrasted. Ergo, a book with purpose materialized. I just had to find the people, interview them, and write up the content in an engaging fashion. A decision was made to focus on the memories of visitors, as opposed to residents, in part because that coincided with my own situation but mostly because I had a hunch that there would be marked difference between visitors and residents. In fact, I had the hunch confirmed. Clare [22] lives in nearby Fairlie and all her life she has visited the Island at every opportunity, whereas her husband was born and brought up there and is somewhat ambivalent about coming over now that he has things to occupy him on the mainland. Figure that one out! The residents' group would be for another day. I had previously written only fiction, but I had spent a career writing up financial reports and proposals, so this was obviously not going to be <u>that</u> different! We shall see!

Getting thirty-two volunteers was not difficult. No advertising was done. No bribes were proffered. Well, a couple of beers but I was thirsty anyway. Of course, the project took place in the middle of a global pandemic just to add a little drama. Potentially it might have made getting together for interviews difficult, if not impossible. No, it did not work out that way, I am glad to say. By inviting folks to wander by our idyllic mobile home on the Island while we were there or hooking up to them all over the world through the technical wizardry of Zoom or Messenger, all the interviews were completed with no problems to speak of. Participants sometimes made preparations in advance, sometimes they just winged it, but in every case once I got them going, it was hard to close them down. The memories flooded back in every case, along with a lot of laughter, as we recognized that each conversation was beginning to fit into a pattern. But enough of that later!

Chapter 2.

A Brief History of Millport and the Isle of Cumbrae

IV The historical tearoom at Fintry Bay.

One of the most captivating sights in the whole world, espoused not just by me but also by most of the participants in this project, is riding on a paddle steamer, preferably The Talisman, as it rounds Farland Point and heads into Millport Bay. Suddenly out of nowhere, the town of Millport emerges, delicately placed on the shores of Great Cumbrae with the two small Eileans standing guard in front of it in the placid---unless they should be roused---waters of the bay. I don't suppose there were lone planners to design the whole town; it evolved over quite a period of time, but if there had been, they would surely have located themselves exactly at the place where the steamer rounds the point in order to design the perfect town! There is a beautiful symmetry about it all---the West Bay a mix of imposing gentrified villas and huddled narrow streets of small flats; the central area of colourful shops and flats with more imposing houses on the hill rising behind them; and all of them sitting on a welcoming promenade with sandy beaches, the East or Kames Bay with arguably the best curved beach, flanked by more imposing villas. The development of the town, which grew out of two separate villages in the west and east, reflects an "us and them" culture which was prevalent in the Victorian Age. The sprawling villas and the modest flats, many consisting only of a single room, remind us of a class division that is no longer in evidence so much today. Hence, most of the villas have now been subdivided and many of the flats have been enlarged by knocking two into one and incorporating that most fundamental of improvements, the inside toilet!

The steamers, with the sole exception of The Waverley, and even she cannot now make that dramatic turn at Farland Point and head toward the old pier, are alas no more. Cumbrae is now accessed by a short, eight-minute ferry ride from Largs to Cumbrae Slip, the two places located directly across from one another, and no doubt thought out by an engineer, who never felt the drama of Farland Point rather than a dreamer, who probably would have. However, once landed on the Island, the 10-minute bus or car ride or the 25-minute cycle or the 80-minute walk, will achieve the next best thing to that steamer arrival. The town will be entered in the East Bay by way of the captivating Lion Rock and academic-looking Field Studies Centre and the road will take you to your desired destination, be it Kames Bay or the front promenade or on to the West Bay. A similar experience will be felt today from that of Victorian times. That is the magic of Millport. Oh sure, changes do occur, but they are subtle and in many ways the place is just as it was over one hundred years ago. Why more costume movies are not shot in Millport I do not know.

It would be wrong to suppose that the beginning of the Island's development dates from then, however. Great Cumbrae, and its little sister island Wee Cumbrae, have been recorded as far back as the 500s and have enjoyed an interesting history in getting to where they are today.

Christianity came to the west of Scotland (as it is now) around 563 through St Columba, and very soon found its way to the two Cumbrae isles. In the following century, two of Columba's disciples, St Maura and St Beya, established a presence on Greater Cumbrae and Wee Cumbrae respectively. There is evidence of both saints to this day. There is also indication, from the 12th century, of Cumbrae Church's affiliation with the significant Paisley Abbey on the mainland. Much of the writing from those early times refers to Cambray or Cimbray or Cimbrae but they are the same places as the Cumbraes of today.

It was Wee Cumbrae that seemed to have the more dramatic history, especially from the 1300s to the 1500s when it had a strong royal ownership and presence. Both Robert II and Robert III, direct descendants of the famous Bruce, frequently occupied the castles on Wee Cumbrae and across the firth at Portencross. The island was a prized hunting ground for the royals as well as productive for farming. Alas, in 1445 John, Earl of Ross, in his ultimately futile attempt to conquer Scotland, laid waste to the ABC islands located together on the Clyde---Arran, Bute, and (Wee) Cumbrae. In the 16th century, the present castle, or more accurately the keep, was constructed by Lord Eglinton who had been granted stewardship of the Island by the crown. More drama ensued when Oliver Cromwell took control of Scotland and had the keep partially destroyed for what appears to be a revenge on the Eglintons rather than for any strategic military value. The shell of the keep remains intact to this day and is well worth a visit.

Gradually, as Great Cumbrae grew in importance, its little sister diminished. The population of the latter island reduced until the few remaining permanent occupants were connected to its strategic location in the firth. Two lighthouses were constructed in the 18th century, the first being the earliest lighthouse on the west coast and with it came the royal intention to keep ships safe in the Clyde and to charge tolls on certain cargos that they carried. The latter lighthouse, located on the edge of the island, was manned until 1974 when it was converted to solar power. It had gone through several phases of changing technology including having the first foghorn in the UK. In a further progressive step, the light was transferred from the original tower in 1997, leaving the interesting but sad relic of a once vibrant lighthouse operation with accommodation for several lighthouse men and families, now deserted but eerily seeming as if it were evacuated only yesterday. It is a pity that a further use for the facilities cannot be found.

The 20th century brought several private owners of Wee Cumbrae but only one, Evelyn Parker, had the wherewithal and inclination to do much development, notably the mansion house and gardens on the east side. Today, the island stands ready and waiting to be utilized for something, probably recreational or tourist related, but the investment necessary does not seem to be available. Informal boat tours have sprung up recently, but once ashore, exploration is heavy going because of inconsistent maintenance and the places of historical significance remain elusive to all but the stout-hearted willing to explore.

The assembly of the different components of the Scotland that we know today took a long time in the first millennium and well into the second. One of the interesting periods was from 870 to 1263, when much of the western islands and part of the mainland was controlled by the Norse invaders. Both Cumbraes fell under Norse rule. Scotland gradually consolidated under one king, and by war and treaty, was able to regain most of its land. However, King Haakon of Norway was unwilling to give up the Cumbraes (well he would be, wouldn't he?) and the matter came to a head at the Battle of Largs in 1263. Although a relatively indecisive affray, it signaled the end of Viking influence; in fact, the Vikings essentially disappeared from Scotland after the Treaty of Perth in 1266. Strong rumour has it that Hakkon spectated on the battle, rather than get his hands dirty or bloodied, from a mound on the Cumbrae side, said to be near the white cottage next to the current water sports centre. In any case, real evidence has been found from time to time of the Norse presence on the Island.

Thereafter, Millport meandered along in its development, unlike its warlike little sister, until the 18th century, when that little matter of tolls and duties on shipping, mentioned earlier in relation to Wee Cumbrae, was to dictate the destiny of Millport. In 1745, there were two very small villages at Kirkstoun and Kamestoun and not very much in between. However, it was apparent to the authorities that administering tolls and duties required a fast cutter to intercept ships plying the Clyde, and Millport was an ideal port, basically in the centre of the firth. The revenue collection function was interesting in those days (one assumes it has changed over the years!); the officers and crew of the cutter were allowed to keep contraband that they confiscated and probably a fair share of the actual tolls and duties that they managed to purloin. Consequently, they became uncommonly wealthy for the age. And they all resided on Cumbrae. Captain James Crawford was able to construct the stately Garrison House and grounds for himself and his officers. The land was leased to him by the Marquis of Bute in an unusual manner. The lease rate was a single rose to be proffered each year on July 11, if requested! Other slightly less ostentatious homes were built by crew members and so began the filling in of the gap between the West Bay and the East Bay. Those collection officers are remembered in posterity to this very day in the street names of Miller, Crawford, Ritchie and others.

Growth of development really exploded in the 1800s because access to the Island became much easier with the invention of the steamship in 1812 by the name of The Comet. With development came the influence of wealth. Ownership of Great Cumbrae was essentially split between Marquises of Bute and the Earls of Glasgow. A pier was first constructed in 1833 making it much easier for steamers to load and unload passengers and cargo. That pier would remain in private hands until 1905 when Millport Burgh Council bought it. More of them later for they were instrumental in the 20th century development in a way that the present-day North Ayrshire Council could only dream!

In 1819 the Earl of Glasgow purchased the Garrison House from the heirs of its original builder, James Crawford. The good Earl was to be responsible for considerable investment and development at that time. In 1851 the Cathedral of the Isles was completed thanks to the largess of a succeeding earl and was to become a focal point of Episcopalianism in Scotland as well as the smallest cathedral in the UK (some said in Europe until some scurrilous counter claims emerged from Serbia of all places).

The Victorian era was the making of Millport. The large villas in the West Bay and East/Kames Bay emerged at this time, often as a result of wealthy businessmen in Glasgow fancying a week-end escape pad on the water. In 1864 Millport became a Police Burgh meaning it had its own court (imagine that!), town council and provost. The Earl of Glasgow was elected/selected as the first provost, which seems fair enough considering all he had done for the Island.

Education was not ignored in this period of rampant growth. Cumbrae Public School was opened in 1876 and in 1897 the University Marine Biological Station, an eminent research facility under the auspices of the University of Glasgow and the University of London, was opened. It remains to this day but has morphed into the charitable trust run Field Studies Centre. A great many school and university students across the UK are well familiar with Great Cumbrae thanks to their research experience. So again, the secret is out!

Beginning at the turn of the century, the great strangle hold that two aristocrats held over the Island began to loosen as the Earl of Glasgow ran into financial problems. Much later, the Marquis of Bute liquidated his holdings in 1999 and for the first-time property owners, including the farm owners, were able to acquire title to their property. There is no understating, however, the importance of the two families in the development of the Island.

With easy access via railways and steamships, the 20th century was the boomtime for Millport. The family holiday emerged from the reduction in working hours brought about by successive labour laws. Eventually, dads were able to take two weeks holiday at the same time as their fellow workers in their city. The Glasgow Fair, Paisley Fair, Edinburgh Trades, and Greenock Fair holidays had come of age. Places like Rothesay, Dunoon and Millport prospered. A tradition emerged of a family renting a place for four weeks and while the mums and children stayed for the duration, the dads enjoyed their two weeks but then had to return to work. However, they would return to the Island the two remaining weekends on the quaintly entitled "daddies' boats"---steamers chock-a-block with fathers headed for piers, where hundreds of mothers and children awaited their re-arrival. It conjures up quite a scene!

The entire infrastructure for summer holidays grew up around Millport. Differing kinds of accommodation, ranging from hotel to boarding house to self-catering home to many a single room with outside toilet, emerged along with shops to serve every conceivable need (well over 100 in the 1920s in this little town) and amusements and activities of every type. The focus of this book is that we will explore the memories of these very things and more.

The Millport Bowling Club came into being in 1871 and even had a Glasgow branch from 1888. It seems that every male visitor, and not a few female visitors, came to play bowls on every day of their holiday. Clubs from the west of Scotland came to compete against the accomplished local team and once per year, an all-star team, comprising players from all the around the mainland, came to play against the local team in the rather grand-sounding extravaganza entitled *Millport versus The Rest of The World*! Golf was not to be left behind, and a club existed from 1888. The present challenging course was laid down by James Braid in 1913, who then proceeded to lead Scotland in an all-star challenge match against England. Honours ended even. Not bad for a wee country, and we are still looking for similar results today!

An exciting and entirely appropriate watersports centre was opened by the government in 1976. Much like the biological station, here was another opportunity for young people across the country to be exposed to the glorious Island while they learned or practiced all manner of water activities from fun stuff to Olympic standard competition. What more could anyone want? Alas, the centre became the victim of government austerity, not to mention short-sightedness, and closed in 2020. At the time of writing, an alternative use, under the auspices of local not governmental control, is still being pursued.

In addition to organized events, and there were tons of them, one of the beauties of the Island experience was the ability to amuse oneself, something we will later explore and there we will see a gigantic difference between the children of the last century and the children of today when no iPad or Xbox was available.

Was it all too good to last?

Throughout the 20th century, the growth of tourism and the development of the Island went together. The basics had to be looked after. Fresh water for the Island was for the longest time obtained from two reservoirs conveniently located by the golf course, in the higher inland area. However, several hot and dry summers in the 1960s (yes, they did happen) caused water shortages, and even the need for it be ferried in, and so a permanent pipeline was installed from neighbouring Bute to ensure continuity of supply (assuming Bute never runs out). A private gas company had established a coal-fired gas works in 1840, which was eventually bought out by the progressive Millport Burgh Council in 1896. That remained the Island's main source of power until it was finally closed by Scottish Gas in 1981, the very last coal-fired gas station to close in the UK. I have dual interests in the concluding history of gas in Millport. I can remember, even in the early 1960s, our boarding house in West Bay still had gas lighting that had to be lit with a taper each evening. I do not recall ever seeing gas lighting indoors anywhere else, except perhaps in films. It just added to the mystique of the place, although I would not fancy ever being asked to light the gas at night. I was very wary of it. That's what dads were for. I also trained as an accountant with Scottish Gas from 1969-1974 and one of my jobs for a while was to make the feu duty payments for all the properties that housed gas works throughout Scotland, including the payment to the Marquis of Bute for Millport. I was kind of proud to be an indirect contributor to the economy of the Island I loved. Little did I know that the same company would yank the service less than 10 years later and not provide a natural gas service in its place. It was goodbye to gas unless you shipped it in by cumbersome bottle! Electricity was brought to the Island in the early 1950s to replace gas and is now taken for granted as the principal means of power. That is until, and if, wind and solar power ever establish a foothold.

That Burgh Council deserves some more mentions in its quest to develop Millport. Before radio, if not newspapers, never mind television and the internet, the Council employed one Jimmy Ferguson as bellringer and town-crier around 1900. What a splendid way to hear the news. I wonder what time (or day) the football results came through! In that same timeframe and in pursuit of its mission to ensure the orderly conduct of life in the burgeoning tourist metropolis, the Council drew up the first regulations concerning donkeys and ponies on the beaches, with equal concern for the welfare of the visitors and the beasts! Finally, in 1912, the town suffered probably the worst storm of record before and since, which caused substantial damage to the seawall, properties beyond it and the pier. By 1929/30, the Council had created a new, more effective seawall further away from the buildings, which also allowed for a better road and promenade and had also restored the pier.

In 1975 when burgh councils were abolished due to reorganization in Scotland, not only was history changed and not necessarily for the better, but a place like Millport lost the familiarity and immediacy of those charged to look after it. The slowdown, and sometimes absence of maintenance, never mind development, is now all too obvious to see.

Back in 1900, the island community greatly benefitted from the opening of the Lady Margaret Hospital, named, no doubt in recognition of a substantial contribution by the family, after the daughter of the 3rd Marquis of Bute. Many tales have been told of treatments, surgeries, and, in particular, births to ensure that visitors and residents alike were well looked after on the island, without ever having to leave it. Alas, the National Health Service (coincidentally the organization I worked in after Scottish Gas!) in seeking efficiencies and economies and possibly improvements, has adopted a policy for many years of centralizing services. Now, though the Lady Margaret is still open, its services are limited in the extreme, as this writer found last year when ambulanced there after a serious boating accident. It was two paracetamols and a call for an ambulance to the mainland! Had I attended after the ferries had stopped running, it would have been on to a helicopter instead of the ambulance, thanks to the provision of a landing pad provided by the local Kerr family. Such is the changing nature of health care.

There remains one more evolutionary step that should be mentioned in getting us to the Millport of today. It is really two, in fact, that have combined. I noted earlier that from around the last decade of the 20th century the numbers of visitors and the kinds of visits changed significantly, causing a challenging future for the hitherto single-industry, holiday isle. Firstly, the dreaded automobile reared its ugly head. There had been no roll-on/roll-off ferries prior to 1972. In fact, it was quite inconvenient to transport a car to the Island by any of the steamers, and as a result Millport, and the road around the Island, were almost bereft of them. One visitor car had been reported and photographed in 1922 but it had not been considered a trend! It was a characteristic of the place that everybody seemed to cherish, and cyclists and walkers benefitted from enormously. After all, it is only 10.25 miles around the Island, and just how much driving could one anticipate doing in a day, never mind two or four weeks? No, it seems cars on the Island were neither called for, nor needed. But the world that existed on the mainland was changing. Soon everybody and their children had cars and seemingly needed to drive to Millport. In 1976, the new 8-minute service from Largs to Cumbrae Slip was to change everything. Then it is only 1.4 miles by the inland road, originally intended only for farm vehicles and the doctor's car, to the centre of town. It can take longer these days to find a parking space than it does to travel from Largs. And having found that space, the average day tripper will not risk losing it, and so that car will not move again until it is time to leave for home! Government policy has been to subsidize ferry travel costs for some intended benefit to those voters who live on islands. The consequence has been an explosion of day trippers to the exclusion of longer-term visitors that is not particularly popular with residents that the policy was intended to serve. Caledonia MacBrayne, the much-maligned ferry operator of whom you will read much here, reports that in 2019 there were 393,410 return journeys between Largs and Cumbrae Slip. That statistic sits uncomfortably with a resident population of about 1,300. Incidentally, there are about 1,300 residences on the Island of which about 30% are second homes. On the latter number, Bronwyn and I stand guilty as charged and delighted about it!

The second step that has influenced the number and kind of visits stretches back to the 1970s and the advent of cheap package holidays to the continent of Europe and beyond. When your mere two weeks holiday could be in guaranteed sunshine it was a severe temptation. When the holiday could be taken for about the same cost as going to Millport as usual, it became a no-brainer. People voted with their feet toward any number of close-by airports and the visit to Millport, if it survived at all for a family, transitioned from a two or four week stay to a day trip once in a while. That was the reality until very recently. Now we are seeing something of a renaissance, as noted earlier with older people, sometimes accompanied by children and grandchildren, starting to make the pilgrimage again. Short-term accommodation rentals are at a premium and the acquisition of second homes is causing prices to skyrocket. Flats that could sit empty and for sale for years are now selling just as soon as they are put on the market. In addition, every cloud has a silver lining and both the real and psychological impact of the global pandemic have reduced visits to countries abroad in favour of the *staycation*. The result of this has been a significant upsurge in daytrips for those fortunate to get on to the ferries and a wasted journey for those not. Where that one will go as the restrictions on travel are gradually eased will be interesting to observe.

That in a nutshell is the history and present of Millport, Isle of Cumbrae. It is simply intended to establish a context for our project ahead. What do thirty-three unrelated visitors remember of this location and the changes it has gone through, while they doggedly exhibit their loyalty to the place where only good things happen?

Chapter 3

How It All Began, Where and When

V The Old Pier, West Bay with Bute and Arran beyond.

This book would not be possible without the invaluable contribution of The Gallant Thirty Twa, to borrow the name of a famous folk song in describing the thirty-two volunteers who shared their memories. Throughout I will refer to a participant by their first name. If you want to know a little about each participant, the number attached to a name will refer to a list of all participants at the back of the book.

Will thirty-two volunteers all think the same way? Highly unlikely, but the fun is in noting where their thoughts do coincide as much as it is when they wildly differ. And do thirty-two similar thoughts point to an irrefutable fact? Maybe yes, maybe no. The point of the book is to share the memories. Readers can decide if their own particular memories resemble what is in the book. My suspicion, now that I have completed the interviews, is there could be much head-nodding and smiling among the readership in recognizing similarities with their own experiences.

Among the participants, I unearthed folks with first memories of visiting Millport stretching from the 1940s through to the 1970s. In addition, there were some with memories from even earlier days, no doubt passed down to them by parents or grandparents, and there were a few relative youngsters with memories only from late in the old century or even from the last twenty years.

Millport is all about family and family tradition. Virtually all the participants began their love affair with the Island by being brought there as a child. In fact, I can only think of one charming exception. Suki[23] first came to the Island in 2009 to follow friends all the way from Glasgow. Not exactly a distant starting point, but previously, she had never heard of Millport! Hers was also a less than conventional arrival…but more of that later. By far the majority of participants fell into a definite pattern---they were brought by their parents in that glorious period for Millport, and on the Clyde in general after World War II, when there seems to have been a widespread desire to rid themselves of the deprivations of wartime and go have some fun again. Furthermore, after the financial hardships of the 1930s and '40s, there was an ability to afford a summer holiday. The relatively short trip "Doon the Watter" was to change the lives of a great many people.

The composition of the family group varied among the participants. While I only ever visited with my mother and father and brother, i.e., two generations, some groups consisted of three generations, as Granny was often included. There might even have been the odd four generational group. Fraser[32] remembers Granny ruling the roost as the senior member of the family present, while Spencer[16] recalls living one time in a house in West Bay opposite the playpark. He and his siblings could play outside for as long as they wanted; that was until Granny strategically placed a copy of the Glasgow Herald in the window. That was the signal to come in, probably for dinner, and it was obeyed immediately. He knew better than to mess with Granny! Other groups might not have been multi-generational but consisted of more than one family, sometimes two or three, all cloistered together in the same location. As we will soon find that location was generally only suited to one very small family. As a variation on the theme, Alison B[27] has fond memories of her family and three aunts and uncles with their children, that is four families in the group, owning four caravans in the Kirkton site, and everyone staying there at the same time each year. She suggested that the children, cousins all, hunted as a pack from morning till night and could easily take over playparks on their own.

This tradition of handing down the practice of going to Millport from generation to generation appears as strong as ever. And that is in spite of the very obvious differences that can be detected between say someone born in the 1940s to someone born in the "noughties". Differences there might be, but an almost inexplicable attraction that is passed on through generations is as strong as ever. Participants will offer their own explanations for this attraction later on.

Perhaps the best story of how a tradition began, because there always has to be someone to begin it, came from Mary[1]. In 1938, her future father-in-law canoed all the way from Ayr to Cumbrae, liked what he saw and took up residence in Millport. Later he became the last harbour master on the Island as well as fostering the family tradition of visiting, a tradition that Mary[ibid] adopted in the 1960s and has maintained to this day.

Particularly in the early days, very few of the participants were fortunate enough to own a property on the Island. Some stayed in hotels and boarding houses (there were over 14 to choose from in Millport in 1960) and tended to stay for weekends or one to two weeks at a maximum. Others rented houses or flats or single rooms of which there were a great many on offer. In this case, there was a tradition for those coming from the west of Scotland to book accommodation for an entire month. Such luxury; the best I ever managed was two weeks! This practice brought about that great institution---the daddies' boat. Mother and children would encamp for the full month, but dad got only two weeks holiday from his employer, and halfway though the month he had to leave to go back to work. Like many other men in the same position, he left on the daddies' boat (the last boat on a Sunday evening). However, come the third weekend of the month, all the men returned on the daddies' boat again (on the Friday evening) to enjoy a little post-script to their holiday. Then once again, they set out for work on the daddies' boat (on the Sunday evening). So many of the participants spoke of bittersweet memories of standing on the pier waving like mad to fathers departing or arriving in this quite quaint manner. I remember one year my own father could only get a single week of holidays and had to leave to return to work in this same manner. Of course, I only thought this turn of events was happening to me personally and was probably some sort of punishment for something I had done. I had no inkling of the daddies' boat and never even noticed all the other children on the pier!

Over the years, particularly during the crazy days after the War and into the '70s, it was quite a task to actually secure a reservation for rental accommodation. Of course, there was no Facebook or TripAdvisor then. Reservations had generally to be made in person and necessitated a visit in the early spring to look for the notices in windows indicating space to rent. That might not have been too much of a hassle for folks living close by who could combine it with a nice little Easter outing. Heaven knows how people from further afield managed. I know we were fortunate in that a temporary booking for next year seemed to be made at the end of the latest holiday. The biggest difficulty was my father securing the necessary time off. Despite being a policeman since the '40s, he appeared to have no control over when he got his holidays. On a couple of occasions, we had to reschedule the temporary reservation but, on at least two other occasions, we were unable to find a suitable alternative time. That meant no Millport that year because my parents never contemplated going to any other accommodation. Talk about the world appearing to come to an end (as we know it!).

The trauma of arranging suitable dates for rental seems to have had a lingering effect on quite a few of the people I spoke with. Some, including Donald & Jennie[11] have never forgotten the stress of being interviewed by the almost invariably crusty landlady to ascertain their suitability to enter the hallowed hall in question. These days nobody can be denied for fear of a charge of discrimination but in those days if your face did not fit, you were out. John[6] remembers exclusion for another reason, the matter of a broken window from the previous year meant he was out. Minia[31] suffered a different setback; reservation was made without problem but when her family arrived at the house to be shared (a not uncommon practice), the owner demanded full payment up front. Annoying but not unheard of, worse was to come when they returned home from a first day at the beach to find themselves locked out, and the owners out on a bender with the proceeds of the rental! All was eventually sorted out with help of the friendly island policeman. Remember this is Millport where only good things happen! Some sadder tales came out of the failure to secure a satisfactory booking, even after the family had visited the Island in numerous prior years and even stayed in the accommodation in question. Several participants reported the unthinkable. Their family decided that after failure to secure a booking there was nothing else for it but to try somewhere else with unlikely names like Rothesay, Dunoon, and Girvan. And worse still in some cases, they never returned to Millport until many years later. But return they must have done, because they are part of my story!

A family deciding to give Millport a miss would have had a traumatic effect on the children (I know from experience), but few would have taken matters into their own hands quite like Bill[18]. But then again, Bill was destined to be something of a trailblazer. When his family opted out of the annual holiday, he decided to simply get there by his own devices, and without spending a penny on the effort. He walked from Denniston to the centre of Glasgow, hitch-hiked to Largs, and persuaded the skipper of a pleasure boat leaving for a cruise, to drop him off on the Island free of charge. There you are---mission accomplished! Throw in a bit of camping on the fly, or wild camping as it is now known, and you have covered travel and accommodation yet still not put your hand in your pocket. I am surprised that more people did not adopt this mode of holidaymaking!

Back to The Gallant Thirty Twa. By hook or by crook, they all seemed to manage to get to Millport, more years than not, especially when they were young. Given the wide array of accommodation available as noted earlier, there was an interesting discernible trend of

21

loyalty, almost loyalty to the extreme. Is that something unique to Island visitors? Let me give you a couple of examples. If a family's choice of where to stay was a boarding house, they did that year after year with no incursion into any alternative type of accommodation. If it was a caravan, it was always a caravan. If it was tiny flat, it was always a tiny flat. There was a distinct loyalty. There was even an almost perverse loyalty to the small flat with an outside toilet. Some ten participants paid homage to the outside toilet they endured every year even when they would not have dreamt of putting up with such at home. That is loyalty!

Another example of loyalty related to the location of their chosen accommodation. If one is inclined to divide the Island into four sectors---it would divide into West Bay, centre of the town, Kames or East Bay, and outside of Millport, I found that participants were fiercely loyal to their location and very seldom strayed from one sector to another (rather like the East Berlin of those same days!). I was a solid West Bay aficionado but later in life wandered into Kames Bay and then the centre. Like the prodigal son, I eventually returned to the West Bay. Well not quite the West Bay; technically out of town in the Firth View Mobile Home Park. That reminds me of Suki[23]. You might remember her arrival on the Island was recent and somewhat later in life. Well, her first accommodation was a tent on the beach at Fintry Bay, initially pitched below the tide line! Her mode of transport into town was a kayak, to be accompanied by a seal. And her later abodes were the Cathedral and the Water Sports Centre. It was only after that she deemed it appropriate to move into town proper.

Her time in the old college accommodation at the Cathedral resonated strongly with me. She reported that she was the only occupant at the time, in a building that tends to be a bit spooky at the best of times. At least she knew in advance that she was the only guest. I once stayed there overnight during one of those ludicrous "When in the neighbourhood, visit Millport" sojourns in the middle of winter. After a jolly night in the pub, I made my way back to the Cathedral in the blackest darkness. Inside was not much better. I felt my way to my room, collapsed into bed and fell asleep, only to be rudely awakened by a ghostly rendering of an operatic aria. Then another…. I did not get up to investigate, but at breakfast the next morning I met the only other guest. He was an opera singer who needed to practise for an upcoming engagement!

Talking about the Cathedral, Josh[17] had quite some tales to tell. His family was part of the Community of Celebration, an Episcopalian group from Texas, USA, who based themselves in the Cathedral dormitory for 10 years from 1975 to 1985 while carrying on Christian outreach work. Josh[ibid] was actually born here in 1980, which makes him a bona-fide Millportonian, albeit with very short period of residence. He has twice visited again, including performing at the Country and Western Music Festival. Although he sounds as true a Texan as any defender of the Alamo, he professes to feel just a wee bit Scottish and in his long-distance conversation with me, he exhibited both a knowledge and a love of the Island worthy of any more frequent visitor including myself. He will contribute to topics later, but I cannot forget his comment about his temporary home in the Cathedral: "It is such a beautiful little church. We don't have little churches like that in Texas. Everything is much bigger!".

I suppose it is inevitable that people would stop visiting the Island almost religiously, as their lives and circumstances changed. Almost a quarter of the participants reported that they followed the trend of giving up visiting for two or four weeks each year and becoming periodic day trippers. That way they could travel elsewhere, usually abroad, and still maintain their loyalty to the little town. However, they have in their own way contributed to the congestion around Millport attributed to the day trippers, but surely that is better than not visiting at all. In contrast, an amazing 41% of the participants have done what I have done. After years of renting accommodation of various types and sizes, they have now bought their own property, the ubiquitous "second-home", and can visit as often and for as long as they like. Tracy[15] may hold the record with a reported average of 34 weekend visits per year! Every one of the new owners exuded a pride in their decision to put down roots on their beloved Island and felt what they owned now was a step up from what they had previously rented. Given that my friend Wilson[8] had told me his rented accommodation as a child amounted to a converted garden shed, the sense of improvement to a luxurious mobile home is all too understandable! That sense of pride in owning now in Millport was never better articulated than by Minia[31]:

"After staying in same boarding house for 12 summers, we decided to buy our own place and we have had it now for 45 years!".

One of the things that made staying in the same accommodation year after year so enjoyable for folks is that they got to know all the neighbours. Both Mary[1] and Tracy[15]noted that the same people came to the adjoining flats and caravans respectively every year. Some even came from the same towns or cities as they did but they only got to know them when they were in Millport. So put that together with the fact that extended families and multiple generations often holidayed together, and you have instant, and often long-lasting friendships, all associated with a particular place they were renting. No wonder people were so keen to secure the same accommodation each year. Mary[ibid] noted there never seemed to be any permanent Island residents in close proximity. They seemed to live somewhere else! And those friendships can indeed last a lifetime. Eileen[13] from New Zealand, told a wonderful story of when she visited the Island after 40 years, walked into Ye Olde Tea Shoppe and who should she meet but her childhood friend who was visiting Millport for the first time in a very long time as well. Karma Millport-style or what!

We have reached the end of recollections about what brought people to Millport and the places that they made home, if only for a short period each year. Undoubtedly those images became embedded in people's minds with pleasure and passed on to succeeding generations so that they might have the same experience. I will close this chapter with a chuckle. Bill[18] who became a famous actor, and the late Kenny Ireland, also a noted actor and director of the Edinburgh Lyceum Theatre, shared not only thespian roots. They were also part of that unique group of children who came each year to Millport for their holidays. Later, when their vocations took them all over the world, each would send the other a postcard from wherever they were and would add a caption: "Doesn't this remind you of Millport?". No chance of them ever forgetting it seems!

Chapter 4

The Thrill of Just Getting There

VI DEPV Talisman in full flow at 17 knots!

The thrill of being on an island cannot be overstated. Any island, be it some remote Atlantic outcrop like St Kilda or the Isle of Cumbrae sitting a mere 1.4 miles from the mainland at its shortest crossing will do the trick! And I always believed that the thrill of being on Cumbrae was evenly matched by the thrill of getting there. It appears that all The Gallant Thirty Twa were in total agreement. How about that!

Glasgow has an inescapable link to Cumbrae. It represents the last of the urban behemoths before transitioning to the serenity of the little jewel of the Clyde. Indeed, whether you live in Glasgow, just outside Glasgow (that common euphemism for what amounts to just about the rest of Scotland), somewhere in the UK, or even somewhere else scattered around the world, the answer is the same---you have to go through Glasgow to complete the journey---at least you did when trains were the preferable mode of transport to cars, and that was not that long ago.

There are two train lines out of Glasgow Central station that facilitate getting to Millport. One terminates at Wemyss Bay and the other at Largs. Why the gap between Wemyss Bay and Largs was never filled in to make a circular track is not known but probably has to do with cost and a strong "not in my backyard" lobby. So, the choice has always been there, take the train to Wemyss Bay or take the train to Largs. We always chose Wemyss Bay. Why, I don't know, but I am glad because it meant a much longer voyage on the steamer and that was a major component of the thrill factor in getting to the Island. Nowadays all that has changed. The steamers have all gone as ferries have replaced them, and the voyage is now that shortest distance possible, the 1.4 miles, the focus being on transporting cars first and foremost. A pity that another one of life's little charms has disappeared in the dubious stumbling march toward progress.

Getting on that train in Glasgow Central was the common step one but for some of us that was after getting to Glasgow Central. Glasgow has two stations. That is most inconvenient. It used to have more but in the move toward consolidation it stopped at two. The two stations are not that far apart but for all those travellers who first had to go Queen Street station, the distance between the two felt like an inexcusable incursion into the quest for Millport. The wealthy might hop into a taxi if they could find one, but for most of us it meant a walk while being forced to carry all the luggage. For me, that probably meant my bucket and spade and whatever chocolate I had not consumed on the earlier train from Edinburgh to Queen Street. The walk probably took 15 minutes, less if I had not stopped to grumble, but felt like at least an hour. Seona & Gordon[5] seemed only to recall taxis between the stations, lucky them! Of course, there was also the challenge for those who actually lived in Glasgow and had to find their way to Central. Bill[18] can recall a tram sometimes and a taxi on other occasions, perhaps depending on current family fortunes, but he did not seem to mind which was mode was taken. The destination was the important thing.

Perhaps I was influenced by the inconvenience of having to carry my own bucket and spade that I somehow implied my family was loaded down with luggage. In truth, that was not the case for my family. Along with most of the other families on the same pilgrimage, we had utilized possibly the greatest invention of the 20th century, which has, alas, also disappeared into the mists of time. I am referring to the trunk, apparently referred to as such by people from the east of Scotland, or the hamper, according to the west. Either way, it was a big receptacle made of wood, metal, or wicker. And, it had previously served another purpose such as a blanket box or ammunition chest or ocean liner trunk. I always suspected ours might even have served as a coffin for a small person. It was kind of creepy! A great invention it was, however. Everything went in the trunk---all clothing except the things to be worn to travel, towels and bedding if required (depending on the type of accommodation that had been rented), pots and pans, plates and cutlery, if required. Also included would be toys, but not too many, in order to create a need for the purchase of new ones in Mapes Toyshop, and a raft of other things that mothers had thought about in advance and would be able to produce mid-holiday when I might have opined with regret that something was probably left at home that I could now do with. The trunk was picked up by the porter from the railway company some days before departure, in our case on the Tuesday, for some others up to ten days prior. There was a certain disadvantage to this. Once clothes were washed and pressed for the holiday, they went into the trunk and were not to be worn again until we got to Millport. That meant very limited attire for me from the Tuesday until the Saturday. Fraser[32] and Donald of Donald & Jennie[11] bemoaned the absence of anything to wear for over a week prior to departure while Bill[18] recalled setting foot on the Island in his school uniform (his only clothes not packed in their trunk) and feeling like Lord Snooty of The Beano fame! That did not last long, as 45 minutes after their arrival, he was changed out of his uniform and set for play thanks to one very good reason. The trunk had arrived at his accommodation in advance of the family. That was the wonderful feature of the service! How the

27

railway company managed to handle the vast number of trunks arriving from all over the country at Wemyss Bay and headed for either of Millport or Rothesay, I don't know. They don't seem to exhibit that same level of competence these days. In spite of the apparent expertise of the porters, however, there were some expressions of caution from participants. Ann and Ian[9] recalled the horror of an event one day on the pier at Wemyss Bay when a trunk unceremoniously slid off the gurney and disappeared into the crystal blue waters of the Clyde (at least they were back then). They joined a mass of passengers standing on the edge of the pier, looking down solemnly, and silently offering a prayer that the trunk was not theirs. It wasn't. Bill[18] confessed to an overriding fear in his family as they witnessed the hustle and bustle of trunk management on the Wemyss Bay pier with an authoritative voice bellowing "passengers for Millport, line up on the left; passengers for Rothesay on the right" (or was it the other way around?) that their trunk would end up in Rothesay and another Paterson family would be enjoying the contents, perhaps even playing with his toys! That fear was always allayed, however, on arrival at their accommodation in Millport when there on the front doormat sat…. the trunk. A great many families must have been grateful for the trunk system which almost did away with the need for any suitcases. That was a good thing because there were no wheels on them in those days. The suitcases had to be lugged. (I wonder if that verb and the noun luggage are related?) Wilson[8] noted that in the event that the trunk could not take all the luggage, some families, his included, simply packed what did not make it into the trunk into the baby's pram. Of course, again in those days, prams were a good deal bigger than today, a bit like comparing an eight-wheeler Albion lorry to a Mazda MX-5. Where baby went in this arrangement, he did not mention! Finally, a couple of people suggested, without being certain, that the trunk travelled free of charge if one purchased one or more passenger tickets so that even car owners, relatively few that there were then, could take advantage of the service. I have been unable to confirm this and suspect it is simply too good to be true.

Before the car ferry came on the scene and more of that to come, the passenger-carrying steamer reigned supreme. And had done for almost 75 years by the time most of participants began to travel and quickly fell in love with this particular mode of transportation.

Each steamer seemed to have its own identity and acquired its own fan club, but none was more loved, it seems, than the DEPV Talisman. It happened to be my absolute favourite as well. The Talisman was a diesel-electric paddle vessel; in fact perhaps the only DEPV, at least, on the Clyde. It was built in 1935 as a prototype of its class, saw some service in WWII, and paddled away until 1953 when it was decided that the experiment was over; it cost too much to run, and it was bound for the scrapper. Fortunately. common sense prevailed a year later when she was transferred to the Wemyss Bay---Largs---Millport run and the love affair began and was to last another 14 years. The Talisman was a majestic lady that glided over the water. Her polished wooden decks were pristine and down below was the spectacle that every father and son cherished---the fully visible engine room with the mighty, thrashing paddles. Probably a few mothers ventured down too with daughters in hand, judging by the upsurge in female marine-engineers that was noted in the years to come!

Wilson[8], Valerie[26], Moira[28], Christine[30], and Fraser[32] all remarked on the joy they felt in arriving at the pier and finding it was to be the Talisman that would ferry them to the Island. There were smaller alternatives you see, that did not offer the same sense of magic. The Talisman with a single funnel was not dissimilar to its two-funnelled contemporary the PS Waverley, that amazingly is still plying those waters on excursion cruises to this day. Many people remark how small the Waverley actually is compared to its photographs where there is no other vessel for comparison. There are some recent photographs that catch the Waverley alongside one of the mega-cruise ships that now use Greenock as a port of call. The contrast in size is astonishing. Well, the Talisman was very similar to the Waverley. Seona & Gordon[5] could never get over just how small she was. And yet, as a child you could wander around the decks endlessly and it felt like you were on a much larger craft. There was something ethereal about the Talisman, whether you were riding on it or standing ashore watching it glide through the water. The previously mentioned climax when it rounded Farland Point and headed into Millport Bay was a joy to behold. As Fraser[32] noted, there was no need for clocks on the Island because people looked for the funnel appearing at the Point and could tell the time with the knowledge of when she due to arrive at the pier. And when the funnels were spotted, there was often a sigh of satisfaction and an acknowledgement that all was well in the world. Nothing can go on forever, unless you are the Waverley and are adopted by a cadre of mad enthusiasts, and unfortunately the Talisman was finally withdrawn from service and broken up in 1967, a wholly inappropriate finale for a fine old lady.There were, of course, many other fine steamers that provided the ferry services to Millport (and various other resorts on the Clyde) or undertook cruises around the Clyde that called in on Millport. Among my participants, favourites were established that folks just did not seem prepared to forget over their lifetimes. Some were older boats, reflective of the age of participants; and some of the newer variety in both cases. In addition, a new demand was placed on the steamers that had scarcely ever been contemplated much. After WWII and into the '60s, people began to acquire cars and wanted to take them on holiday. That meant they wanted to ship them to the holiday islands and other areas such as Dunoon, which were more accessible by water than road. For some reason, Cumbrae fell into that category. I could understand people wanting to drive on Arran, even on Bute, but Cumbrae---10.25 miles, barely enough time to get into top gear. And if you did, you ran the risk of missing some of the sights to be seen around the Island. Steamers had to be modified to accommodate a small number of cars at any one time. And the accommodation was frequently one of improvisations, from cranes, to lifts and turntables, and side and stern loading ramps. Sometimes cars made the perilous trip from ship to shore on two strategically placed wooden planks--- reasonably negotiable on a calm day but something else when the swell got up! It was not uncommon for a nervous driver to hand the keys to a crewmember and walk off by the gangplank. It was inevitable that the demand for cars would get greater and greater every year and alternatives would have to be sought. No replicas of the Forth Road Bridge were ever forthcoming for the islands but something was on the horizon for Cumbrae. More of that to come.

There are a number of books that provide detailed histories of the Clyde steamers, some majestic and some not so much, and I cannot hope to do them justice in a mere chapter. So, if your interest is piqued, I would highly recommend them. But I should mention some boats because of the connection to Cumbrae, be it service to the Old Pier or cruising via the Keppel Pier. The Duchess of Fife had a very long, distinguished career on the firth from 1903 to 1953, including sterling service at Dunkirk in WWII. In an odd decision, the Caledonia Steam Packet Company, operator at the time, assigned her to the Millport service run for 1951-52, i.e., when she was an elderly lady. Both Anne & Ian[9] and Bill[18] remember her with great fondness. I seem to remember my father also making a favourable comparison of her to the Talisman, which was rare praise indeed. The Queen Mary II (1933-77), which went through some name juggles with the Cunard transatlantic liner of the same name, was well remembered for cruises by John[6]. Of that same era, the Marchioness of Graham (1936-57) was recalled by Donald & Jennie[11] and Peter[12] as one of the early vessels capable of carrying cars, but not in the customized manner that was to come later. She primarily served the Isle of Arran but also put in service to Millport. In a similar vein, the Glen Sannox (1957-89), one of four Clyde steamers to bear the name, replaced The Marchioness of Graham for the Arran run and also put in service to Millport. She was a custom-built car ferry and remembered by John[6], Donald & Jennie[11], and Moira[28]. But in a sad postscript, noted by them, the new, fourth Glen Sannox that was all but constructed and scheduled for launching in 2017, remains on the stocks in its Greenock shipyard to the time of writing. Surely that is the most glaring example of governmental confusion on how to provide an effective fleet and operate it on the Clyde and elsewhere in Scotland's coastal waters. Contrastingly, a flurry of activity occurred in shipbuilding in the post-war years. The four Maid boats, namely Argyll, Ashton, Cumbrae, and Skelmorlie, were built in 1953 as fast passenger crafts and lasted until the late 1960s as remembered by Alison R[7]. Their deployment seems to have been interchangeable but at least some of them served Millport at one time or another. I remember them as somewhat charmless vessels and no comparison to the Talisman! In the following year 1954, the custom-built car ferries---Arran, Bute, and Cowal (not Cumbrae which would have completed the set!) came on the scene to meet burgeoning demand for car transportation as recollected by Lorraine[2], Seona & Gordon[5], and Donald & Jennie[11]. It is interesting to note that the service to Millport was only three days a week, with a fourth day being added when required, and photographs of the town in the 1960s still show cars in the minority and bicycles

31

prevailing with pedestrians even having the temerity to wander along the promenade on the road. Wilson[8] mentioned that as late as in the 1970s, people seemed reluctant to bring cars to the Island, even if they owned them. Consequently perhaps, during the 1960s through to the early 1990s, a passenger only service was operated between Largs and Millport and boats that plied the waters---Ashton (1938-65), Leven (1938-65), Countess of Breadalbane (1952-71), and Keppel (1967-93) ---were thought of fondly by many of the participants (Sandra[10], Donald & Jennie[11], Liz[14], Bill[18], Susan B[19], Valerie[26], and Christine[30]). The Talisman had gone but these much smaller crafts could handle the sometimes-choppy waters and occasionally added some excitement by entering Millport Bay between the Eileans just to get everyone's holiday off to a flying start. The Keppel, in particular, seems to have retained a place in people's hearts, including John[6], Alison R[7], Susan B[19], Mark C[25], and Christine[30]. The little lady can still be seen strutting her stuff on the island of Malta as is noted every year by Millport fans venturing further afoot for a change. But the days of service to the Old Pier were coming to an end. Government policy was passenger-only vessels should be phased out and only car ferries should populate the entire fleet in the future. That meant a dramatic change for Cumbrae.

Largs had become a ferry terminal to Cumbrae and calling place for cruises, once the railway station was opened in 1885, to provide a link from Glasgow. From 1890, the Caledonian Steam Packet Company took over the ferry services on the Clyde from several private operators. I suppose the CSPC was an early version of a QUANGO, i.e., it was publicly funded but operated on a quasi-autonomous basis. Things continued in the same way through to the early 1970s when two dramatic changes occurred which would greatly impact the service to Cumbrae. In 1972, a brand-new service began between Largs and the newly constructed Cumbrae Slip, directly across on the Island. And in the following year, Caledonian MacBrayne (the famous or infamous CalMac) was created when the CSPC and David MacBrayne (the ferry operator in the Outer and Inner Hebrides) were merged. The 50-year history of the short, eight-minute, ferry service has been a bumpy one and not always caused by the weather! The early ships, including Coruisk, Largs, and Kilbrannan were not ideally designed for the service needs and were prone to frequent breakdowns. Nevertheless, the new service quickly caught on because visitors (as well as residents) could bring their cars to and from the Island. However, the car capacity on each ferry was limited to six and a new phenomenon, the vehicle line-up, on both sides of the water, came into being. Things improved when the new ferry, MV Cumbrae, imaginatively named by the schoolchildren in Millport, was introduced. She had a capacity of 18 cars and generally ran very efficiently. However, when changes were made in the mid- '90s and the Loch Striven and Loch Linnhe were redeployed to the route, the improved services seemed to slide backwards. Frequent mechanical breakdowns and cancellations for other reasons tended to blight the services. In 1997, the Loch Riddon replaced the Striven and the following year the Loch Alainn replaced the Linnhe without either making a great impact. However, finally in 2007 the brand-new Loch Shirra, with a 36-car capacity, replaced the Alainn and while at first the service improved, it was not sustained. We are now fifteen years on, and those two same ferries continue to struggle to meet the ever-increasing demands while suffering increasingly frequent mechanical breakdowns…and striving to accommodate a global pandemic by applying restrictions that seemed only to apply to this humble little ferry route. Not surprisingly, there has been an ever-escalating division of opinion on the performance of CalMac and, by extension, that of the Scottish Government. Not a week seems to pass without an incident affecting service and the reasons seem to get more and more bizarre.

Most of The Gallant Thirty Twa have lived through the transition from the CSPC to CalMac and have sat in ferry line-ups, feeling their lives go by unfulfilled. They were not shy in identifying the ferry service as perhaps the greatest challenge to managing their desired dual existence of main home (somewhere in Scotland) and second home (on the Island). Notably, Wilson[8] made the case for the Government putting the ferry service to competitive tender in the hope that Western Ferries, which already serves several routes around the country, could be given an equal opportunity to win the contract. Donald & Jennie[11] among others felt CalMac was badly lacking in its public relations and did not exhibit the charisma of its predecessor the Caledonian Steam Packet Company. Tracy[15] also echoed the sentiments of others when she criticized the CalMac service but expressed sympathy for the crews which tend to bear the brunt of the public's frustrations during service interruptions. It is fair to say that it may be many a day before the desired solutions to the ferry problems can even be agreed upon, never mind achieved.

Of course, out of every hardship there tends to emerge a hero to save the day. It would be remiss of me not to mention the late Stewart McIntyre, a renowned private boat operator and entrepreneur on the Island. Alison[7] noted that whenever the ferry did not run for whatever reason or stranded passengers had been left behind after the last scheduled sailing, Stewart would step in and transport folks to the mainland in his own boat. And he would do it without accepting any compensation. How do I know this story to be true? Because I was one of the recipients of his largesse in 1974 when he rescued my family and me from the Island during a ferry strike and I was due to start a new job in Edinburgh the following week!

Such tales of horror concerning the ferry service might prompt the hope that a totally alternative means of getting to Cumbrae is worth praying for. It is not going to be a bridge in anybody's lifetime, and it appears it is not going to be a hovercraft. Twice in the past, in 1965 and again in 1970/1, it was attempted from Largs to Kames Bay beach in the former and to the Old Pier in the latter. Neither succeeded for various reasons---noise, municipal disputes as to whether beaches were free to use, disparity between costs and revenues, mechanical breakdowns (yes them too), and limitations in inclement weather (that too). Susan M[4], John[6], and Liz[14] each had fond memories of the hovercrafts, although only Liz actually ever rode in one, which at the end of the day was the problem---insufficient passengers.

As we leave this chapter that examined the joys and tribulations of actually getting from home on the mainland to this little Island, I cannot forget some of the classic stories and comments that came out of my conversations, and one can only assume that they would only ever occur in the quest to make it to Millport and nowhere else in the world!

- Remembering with fondness, and probably just a little nervousness, the days when it was just too rough for the steamer to make it to the Old Pier and the voyage had to be terminated at Keppel Pier. (Sandra[10])

- The ferry from Millport, probably the Talisman, racing the ferry from Rothesay to Wemyss Bay, not because the pier could not handle two steamers at the same time, but to give the winning passengers first dibs on the seats of the waiting train headed to Glasgow. (Donald & Jennie[11])
- "At the conclusion of WWII, I witnessed the blowing up of defence boom that stretched from Hunterston across to Keppel. I was able to retrieve a dead cod from the water!" (Peter[12])
- "As we drove to Largs to catch the ferry, there was great excitement when we were able to catch a glimpse of the Island through that gap in the wall at the top of the Haylie Brae!" (Donald & Jennie[11] and Clare[22])
- Upon arrival at Cumbrae Slip, it is their avowed and solemn practice to turn right and approach Millport from the back of the Island, unlike 99% of the other drivers who turn left. (Amanda[21] and Suki[23])
- "When we got on the steamer at Wemyss Bay, there was always a seagull perched up at the bow, which would accompany us to Millport. Our dad insisted this was Charlie the Seagull and he would always be there for us. He always was. My sister and I bought china seagulls and have them to this day!" (Moira[28])

Chapter 5

Monuments and Look-Alike Rocks

VII The unmistakable Lion Rock.

The island of Great Cumbrae may only be 4.5 square miles in size but it contains an amazing number of natural rocks that form recognizable shapes or have had a touch of make-up applied in order to take on notable appearances. The geological events over the millennia seem to have almost deliberately contributed to the distribution of interesting rock formations on the 10.25-mile perimeter road that skirts the seashore all the way around the island. It is for that reason, among several, that the bicycle is the favoured mode of transport over the car. The rider can marvel at the sights as they are slowly approached and can even hop off and examine them without any concern about finding a parking space! The hardier visitors, and there are plenty of them, will even forgo a bike and slowly amble around the road on foot. There can be no better four hours, plus allowance for stops, to be spent anywhere in Scotland.

I suggest we undertake the round-island tour together to examine the monuments and look-alike rocks. We will set off from the pierhead, as if we have just disembarked from the early afternoon steamer. Wherever one makes a start on a circular walk, one is faced with the immediate question of whether to turn left or right, ergo to head in a clockwise direction or counterclockwise. All visitors must first go through this decision-making. And judging by the comments of many of the participants, once the decision is made it is followed religiously on every subsequent circumnavigation of the Island. I was always a clockwise person for one good reason---the distance from where I lived as a child in Kimberley House, West Bay, to the ice cream-offering café at Fintry Bay was shorter by that route. Therefore, we will head up Cardiff Street and turn left onto West Bay Road.

The first phenomenon we encounter is in West Bay Park beyond the football field. There, embedded in a stone wall and almost underground is an old canon. A WWI 155mm German howitzer to be precise. Why is it on the Island? There are a few theories. It was one of a pair which were distributed to Millport like other towns as spoils of war; or it was installed as part of the Island defence in WWII (unlikely); or it was used in the training of local volunteers as in Dad's Army. Why was it buried? Possibly to save it being scrapped during WWII when any sort of metal was in demand; or the islanders got fed up with the valueless prize of war and just decided to bury it, giving it a different fate to its partner which was alleged to have been dumped in the sea. This is all good Island legend and not the last one we will find. Both Liz[14] and Donald of Donald & Jennie[11] remarked that they have been visiting the Island from the '50s and '60s respectively and yet only became aware of the canon's existence recently on social media and were then able to witness it for themselves. In all likelihood, reading

37

about it first is the more productive way to find it. There must be thousands of visitors who have crossed the football field, stared at the well-preserved stone wall and then probably looked further on toward that eyesore in many opinions that is Hunterston Nuclear Power Station without ever looking down at the base of the wall to spot the mysterious canon!

As we continue our walk, before we encounter Fintry Bay, we will come upon the relatively new poignant memorial to the merchant seamen lost in the two world wars. Almost all circumnavigators stop at the memorial because it possesses an incredible view toward Kilchattan Bay and the Isle of Bute. Some will even read the inscription and pause to think, as was suggested by Sandra[10].

We have now passed Fintry Bay, after the obligatory ice cream at the splendid new café which has replaced the quaint refreshment bar that was for years operated by "Irish John" Kennedy and continue to head toward the top of the Island, which is probably due north. If we can tear our eyes away from looking over the water toward Mount Stuart House, the ancestral home of the Marquises of Bute and the point beyond which Rothesay Bay would unfold, and instead cast our eyes inland to the rocky headland that fringes the road, what is it that we spy? It is the face of a North American Indian, formed naturally in the rock and highlighted with judicious use of brightly coloured paints. Even in these days of utmost political correctness, its name continues in every tourist publication. It is the Indian Rock. It is suggested that it was first painted in the 1920s by Fern Andy (Sullivan), something of a hermit, who lived in summertime in a cave near Fintry Bay and used local plants to weave baskets and mats, which he sold to visitors. In wintertime, he retired to warmer accommodation in Millport! Every last participant recalled that their walking tours and cycling trips involved stopping and staring at the brightly-coloured brave. It is just a ritual that is not so easily managed from a moving car, as I might have mentioned previously. Valerie[26], although she is now resident in Canada and has not set foot on the Island since the 1980s, was just as able as everyone else to enthuse about the Indian Rock and the fact that it was created, or at least embellished, by Fern Andy. That is how legends sustain.

We have now reached the top of the Island and Largs has come into view on the right. There is an imposing monument on the shore that all cyclists and walkers stop at, but probably just for a bit of a breather. It commemorates the 1844 drowning of two young midshipmen from HMS Shearwater in a borrowed sailboat accident, but it is not a well-known story, unlike many of the other Cumbrae tales. In fact, the details can vary from teller to teller. Although there was an open invitation, not one of The Gallant Thirty Twa referred to the monument. Perhaps, it is just a case of being taken for granted.

We pass the Cumbrae Slip with just a fleeting sideways glance and carry on in the direction of Millport. A leisurely journey can be instantly upended if a ferry has just disgorged a fleet of vehicles headed in the same direction and thinking of the parking issues that lie ahead. We will stop at the wishing well, which is a natural spring that flows out of the embankment under the road and onto the shore. This place resonates strongly with the participants. A number, including Susan M[4] recall it as one of the requisite stopping points on a cycle trip, particularly for those riding in a counterclockwise direction! For it was the place to drink some cool fresh water from the cup provided. Yes, a metal cup attached to a chain was there. The metal might have been iron or steel or pewter even and had a tendency to give off a strange taste if your lips touched it, something not forgotten by Seona & Gordon[5] or Valerie[26]. The water continues to flow to this day, but the cup has long since disappeared, which is probably just as well because otherwise some Brussels bureaucrat would have made it happen! The well was not just the welcome provider of refreshing sustenance; it was also a place to make wishes (that would invariably come true because this is Millport after all). Wilson[8] and Christine[30] were not the only people that clearly recalled the deliberate ceremony involved. A pebble had to be found in the stream that ran across the shore, held tightly in the hand whilst a wish was made; then it was carefully placed with the other pebbles on the rock wall above the pipe that carried the water. Judging by the pebbles in abundance, the process is followed to this day.

Just a little bit along the road, the dramatic outline of the Lion Rock suddenly bursts upon us. This natural geological phenomenon dates from about 65 million years ago (unless one is inclined to believe the alternative tale of it being constructed by a group of demons in competition with a group of faeries who were engaged in the construction of a bridge to the mainland---now there is an idea!) and most definitely reminds one of a prowling lion from either angle. Christine[30] was able to identify the composition of the rock as basalt because her mother, the illustrious Peggy Macrae of whom we will hear more later, was a geology major and "…never missed an opportunity to pass the sacred knowledge on". Whereas Amanda[21] expressed a lifelong fascination with the creature, which was largely prompted by tall tales that her father shared with her (perhaps involving demons and faeries?). Clare[22] also had an imaginative father to thank for stories about the Lion's association with the Underworld. Although it might be actively frowned upon in these days of endless rules concerning health and safety, the climbing of the rock was a strong memory for some. Bill[18] positively glowed at the memory of conquering the beast and recalled with pride that his name was etched at the top in 1952 to record the successful ascent. Presumably it remains there to this day though I suspect he might not be prepared now to climb and verify it! Kyle[24] was another who took pride in recalling how he clambered it from one end to the other. Mark K[20] also had happy memories of assailing the Lion but recalled with some trepidation the overgrown stinging nettles that guarded its base. However, a quick application of docken leaves (Rumex Obtusifolius if you prefer) was just the thing to ease any stings. Now, I remember as a child sustaining the stings and being saved by the docken leaves. The question is would I know how to locate docken leaves today? Would Mark K? To end this treatise on climbing, I feel I have to note the profound, but regretful observation made by Moira[28], that it sounded like a lot of fun but, alas, "…only boys climbed…."! Whether that remains true today, legally or factually, I will not hazard a guess.

As we pass by the Field Studies Centre, the Marine Biological Station as was, there is an instantaneous (and barely that!) opportunity to look up on the cliff face and see the readily recognizable profile of Queen Victoria. It is as clear as day but look up one step too early or one step too late and it is just a plain clump of rock. I have to confess that this seasoned visitor only learned of its existence from social media in recent years and it took me many attempts to reveal it at the exact angle required. I assumed that the likeness had only recently been discovered by everybody else but no, it has long been known about, just not publicized as much as the Indian Rock, Lion Rock, or another rock we are coming to. Peter[12], one of the senior participants, could recall the Queen (her profile in rock I stress) from his childhood but Liz[14], Susan B[19], and Alison B[27], all like me long time visitors, reported that they had only become aware of its existence in recent years but were now confirmed spotters. Alas, Bill[18] confessed that in spite of knowing about it for a long time, he has never been able to make it out on the rock face. A case of walking too fast and not knowing just when to stop and look up! I suppose some make-up enhancement would assist the visibility, but it would be jolly difficult to apply.We are now on Marine Parade in Kames Bay, the scene of a little-known edifice that Wilson[8] raised but had no knowledge of its origin. I was intrigued and took on the role of investigator. I was able to locate, at the west end of Marine Parade, an odd-looking piece of a stone building looking a bit like the remains of a castle or keep, just as the road straightens out. I have found no reference to it in any publication but from a neighboring resident I was able to obtain some information. Apparently, there is a similar building further along the road (although I was unable to locate it) and the two, appearing almost like bookends, indicate the extremities of an old estate which was presumably walled. Wilson[ibid] has obviously unearthed another Millport mystery of which much will be said in the future, just not by me today!

We are now into the town of Millport, but we will step out again by taking the Ferry Road toward the centre of the Island. On the right, in the Gouklan Wood at the far corner, rests the Gouklan Standing Stone. It is about six feet tall and resembles many such standing stones scattered around Scotland and dating from pre-Christian times. In fact, it is said to be the last remaining stone from a circle of three or five stones. Unfortunately, it did not attract a good deal of interest among the participants although most knew roughly where it was. I remember being aware of it for quite some time but never being able to find it. That was all changed when a fine purveyor of the local history, the late Sandy Morton, revealed it to me. The only hassle was the woods were impenetrable and it could only be reached by climbing over a barbed wire-topped wall! I am glad to say that these days the plantation has been thinned out and several paths lead to the standing stone, alone in all its majesty.

We are bound for the Glaidstone, the highest point on the Island, and just before we reach it, we see another well, this one more formally structured than its counterpart on the shoreline. It was actually constructed in 1929 by an entrepreneurial council member to offer the health-invigorating natural mineral water from a nearby spring. Once opened with great ceremony, however, it quickly fell out of favour when the local doctor opined that more benefit was likely to be gained from the walk up to the well than would ever be derived from drinking the suspect water out of the metal cup provided (another of those cups!). This well appears to have dried up now, although Wilson[8] could recall drinking from it as a child. Its demise is a pity because it is thirsty work walking or cycling up to the top of the Island. The Glaidstone does not appear to have any great historical significance but every visitor (and resident for that matter) will make the effort to get there because the 360° view is to die for.

We are now heading back into the town by way of College Street with the Cathedral on the left and the Garrison on the right, both to be explored in detail later. Once we turn left onto the promenade, there it is in all its glory---the pièce de résistance of all monuments and look-alike rocks on Cumbrae---the Crocodile Rock. Around 1913, it is pretty reliably recorded in the burgh council annals that one Robert "Tadger" Brown, upon emerging from the Tavern bar after a lunchtime refreshment or two, looked across at a rock sticking out of the water and swore it reminded him of a crocodile. He later returned with brushes and paints to embellish the rock so that everyone else could see what he saw---this fierce crocodile thrusting its head out of the water at high tide or the languid reptile reclining on the beach at low tide. And every year for more than 100, the Croc Rock's make-up has been redone because he is, without a doubt, the most photographed thing on the Island. In any survey, it is highly unusual to get absolute unanimity on any topic. However, thirty-two of The Gallant Thirty Twa stated that the Croc Rock is an icon of Island life that is portrayed on just about anything that can take an image, the latest being the home-grown gin bottle. And almost half the participants commented that they have photographs of family perched on the Croc from every single visit made to the Island. The rest were probably no different but just did not want to own up to it. If it were possible, it would be very interesting to know just how many family photographs of the Croc exist around the world! During the high season, even if the sun is not shining, you will see a cluster of people around the Croc waiting their turn to take their photographs. There is no embarrassment or self-consciousness, drunk or sober, about sitting on the reptile and just grinning! Susan B[19] remembered children in her family always referring to "Uncle Croc" so surely, he was a pretty tame reptile. However, Mark K[20] recollected the dangers of trying to manoeuvre oneself into the beast's mouth for the ultimate photograph. Clare[22] remarked that her collection of Croc family photographs was her way of tracking the growth stages of her children. That is literally of course. Figuratively, visitors to Millport, adult or child, never grow up! Bill[18] probably has good reason to have lots of photographs in which he features, given his acting career, but he professes that he features in more Croc pictures than anything else in his life. Maybe it led to him getting his big break!

Finally, we must finish with a great Crocodile Rock story from Donald & Jennie[11]. A friend or relative of theirs with strong Millport connections was on an important business trip to the United States. He had responsibility for negotiating and securing a contract for his company and was nervous about meeting the potential partner for the first time. He was not sure he would be able to pull off the contract. He need not have worried when he walked into the huge office and faced the other businessman seated at an imposing desk with a large photograph behind him. You guessed it---a photograph of the Crocodile Rock!

Chapter 6

Spotting Celebrities

VIII Duncan Macrae filming on the Island.

I said at the beginning of this book, I started out thinking Millport was a wonderful secret, known only to me. Later I found that lots of people held the same secret; in fact it was not much of a secret at all. Now it is obvious that a great many celebrities from all areas of stardom are in on the secret as well and hold the Island dear to their hearts. What is neat about this is, despite their fame permitting them to travel almost anywhere they feel like, celebrities, past and present, have developed the habit of frequently returning to the Island. Some have even made homes here. And many have done it because they feel they can escape the constant spotlight and just be themselves along with all the other visitors, who often do little more than just sneak a quick look at them and try to remember where they recognize that face from!

The Gallant Thirty Twa came up with a grand number of celebrities they had sighted, and, in all probability, they just scratched the surface. Seldom does a week go by on social media that a new celebrity is not linked to the Island and prompts a widespread discussion of what brought them here. The most notable celebrities seem to come from the arts world, the music world, and to a lesser extent the sports world. This representation one might expect, but it leaves in question the absence of other groups such as politicians, businesspeople, religious leaders or royalty. It can only be assumed that they have missed the calling!

The two celebrities most mentioned by participants, by far, were actually couples---Duncan Macrae and his wife Peggy Macrae and Archie McCulloch and his wife Kathie Kay. In fact, either couple could have served in place of the absent royalty such was the esteem in which they were held. Duncan Macrae got his start on the stage when he joined the Glasgow Citizens Theatre in 1943 and he gradually established himself in stage, radio, television and films. Not many movies of that time with any Scottish connection do not include his "weel-kent" face at some point in the story. In 1959, he had the starring role in the first television series of Para Handy, the couthy tales of a Clyde puffer and its very individualistic crew members. Perhaps he was inspired by the show's settings because he, his wife and two daughters, set up shop in Millport as their alternative home to Glasgow. And not only did Duncan assume the mantle of the "Laird of the Island" (OK the shepherd's crook he brandished did help!) but Peggy was to make a huge mark on the community by being the very first special needs teacher appointed in the local school, helping establish the Cumbrae Queen celebrations, and serving with distinction as a Millport town councillor. I remember seeing Duncan and his two daughters on the Hunter/Mauchline quay in the very early '60s. He was leaning on the famous crook contemplating life by way of watching the little boats-for-hire. The girls were just standing there, totally cool, all long straight hair and dark outfits, probably transitioning from the beatniks to the early hippies! Understandably, the fondest memories of Macrae family life on the Island came from daughter Christine[30]. The yarns that she related were a joy to hear and illustrated just how fortunate she and her late sister, Ann, were to grow up in an almost dichotomous setting of exciting showbusiness in the big city and endless fun on the idyllic island. Duncan might have played many roles of a laid-back nature (even before the term was first coined) but Christine[ibid] suggested that he adopted that stance whenever he was present on the Island and be the weather rain or shine, it didn't matter. She remembers, as other remarked, he was an avid swimmer in Kames Bay, where the water can scarcely be described as balmy. In addition, she noted her father's fondness for just hanging out at the Old Pier and watching the goings-on around the puffer Saxon and that undoubtedly prepared him for the role of Para Handy. Furthermore, she had great tales to share of her mother, Peggy, who was a strong personality in her own right and seems to have had a lasting devotion to the Island. As well, Peggy seems to have been the one responsible for furnishing the wooly swimwear among the family to combat the icy waters of the Clyde. That must have done the trick. I am surprised the fashion never caught on! Susan B[19] and Moira[20] were both neighbours of the Macraes in Kames Bay and recall having conversations with them. Fraser[32] was also a neighbour and remembers Duncan bursting forth from the house, waving to them, racing across the putting green and onto the beach and with no hesitation into the frigid water. After a while he would emerge from the water and retrace his steps, his skinny frame barely holding up the now water-logged wooly trunks with the assistance of a leather belt, give a wave again to his neighbours, and disappear into the house! Minia[31] had a great fondness for singsongs, of which there appeared to be quite a number in various establishments along the front of the town, and recalled the Macraes joining them along with Andy Stewart and Kathie Kaye in the Supper Room of the Clifton Board House. There must have been a fair amount of professional talent in those particular singsongs. Finally, Bill[18] tells a great story that perfectly sums up Duncan Macrae and his association with Millport. The man was at the pier to meet his friend and fellow thespian Stanley Baxter. Baxter could not spot him in the customary thronging mass meeting the

steamer, until he finally heard the dulcet tones announce, "over here!".
The crowds parted to allow the celebrities to meet. As they strolled
slowly along the promenade toward Kames Bay, Duncan would stop
every few yards to shake hands and speak with residents and visitors
alike. Quite a while later, they finally reached their destination and
Duncan turned to Stanley and said, "You know the best thing I like
about this place is I can be anonymous here!".

Archie McCulloch (1912-97, both Glasgow) had a long career
as a writer, impresario, and broadcaster. He was one of the founding
fathers of Scottish Television and was responsible for its glittering
celebrity launch in 1957, although some may say that was its peak and
it has all been downhill ever since! Kathie Kay was born in Lincolnshire,
England in 1918 and passed away in Largs in 1986. She had a stellar
career as a band vocalist and solo singer, the most notable stint being
starring in the Billy Cotton Band Show on radio and television in the
1950s and '60s. They married and had three sons and established a
second-home base on Cumbrae. They lived for most of that time in the
white cottage near what became the Cumbrae Slip (Anne & Iain[9] and
Donald & Jennie[11]). While acting as the Island's first couple
(apparently, he served as provost of the town), their biggest claim to
fame was owning and establishing the Cumbrae Club, which sought to
be a sophisticated nightclub the likes of which is more generally
associated with much larger communities. For a while, the Cumbrae
Club was the focal point of entertainment in all of Millport. Wilson[8] was
one who also remembered the junior section of the club that was
reserved for youngsters and was a popular haven on a wet day. Liz[11]
also has fond memories of the Cumbrae Club and even worked there
as a means of funding her summer-long holidays. I have to confess that
the club was elusive to me; I associated it only with adults and was
unaware of the junior section. That is a pity that will never be rectified,
for the building has since disappeared and was replaced by modern
flats. The couple seemed to be well known to everyone, as confirmed
by the participants, because they were very accessible. Moira[28] was
one of a number that was proud to have made their acquaintance
through her father. Bill[18] also remarked that their off-island fame helped
to establish their legendary status on-island. He believed that Kathie
Kay had appeared on the Ed Sullivan Show in the US long before the
"you-know-whos" did in 1964. Finally, their youngest son Ken

McCulloch must have been paying attention to how hotels and boarding houses were run on the Island because he went on to have a very successful career as a hotel developer and founded the Malmaison chain of sixteen hotels and the Dakota chain of five hotels that were at the forefront of the boutique hotel movement.

Other celebrities from the world of the arts that came up in discussions with the participants included Larry Marshall, Stanley Baxter, David Tennant, Gavin Mitchell. John Byrne, Kenny Ireland, Bill Paterson, John Barrowman and sister Carole, Gordon Jackson, and Emma Thompson and her mother Phyllida Law. All these artists seem to have been regular or irregular visitors to Millport and I was regaled with interesting stories. Although I was unable to confirm it, Eric[3] was of the firm belief that Larry Marshall was a frequent visitor on his boat and that it may actually have caught fire in the bay one time. Marshall, of course, was one of the earliest personalities on the fledgling Scottish Television previously mentioned. Stanley Baxter's mother brought the children to the Island to escape the bombing of Clydebank in WWII, as noted by Anne & Iain[9] and Bill[18]. Stanley remembered the idyllic life where things were not so strict and there was no homework from the local school! Even after becoming the well-known actor, comedian, impressionist and writer that he is, he has always had time for Millport. While there are no known recordings of Parliamo Millporto, the idea was obviously transferrable to the larger metropolis! David Tennant appears to have been a regular visitor as a child and even to this day. When not playing Dr Who among many other characters, he has found time to visit and unwind. His early days were in the company of his father, The Very Reverend Sandy McDonald, former Moderator of the General Assembly of the Church of Scotland but much more famous for being the organizer of the Seaside Mission, held daily on the sands of Kames Bay! (Eileen[13], Spencer[16], Clare[22], Christine[30], and Minia[31]) Apparently, David assisted his father in this popular activity in the 1980s, which was after my time of attending, though I have to stress I attended not necessarily to broaden my beliefs but rather to catch the sweeties that were liberally distributed for answers remotely connected to the truth! In fact, Spencer[16] recalled not paying attention to the frenzy of answers being yelled out by the audience and being hit on the head by a batch of sweeties intended to be thrown to someone else! Mark K[20] remembered the Seaside Mission well but confessed to a rebellious streak in that while his pals attended the session, he played putting on the adjacent links! Liz[11] and Kyle[24] were among others who claimed a positive sighting of David from more recent times while Tracy[15] was agog to see him enjoying an ice cream in the Ritz Café, which is of course a perfectly natural thing for a Hollywood star to do as we will discover later on! Clare[ibid] noted that even as a child, David was able to attract the attention of the fairer sex and was obviously destined for big things. Gavin Mitchell is a well-known actor and comedian, memorable for playing Boaby the Barman in Still Game. He is also an avowed Millport fan. Tracy[15]and Amanda[21] remarked on the frequency of his visits, and he has mentioned in interviews his joy at being able to relax on the Island and not infrequently in the Tavern! Bill[18] recollected John Byrne and Kenny Ireland and their respective associations with Millport. John is an accomplished playwright with many titles to his name including Tutti Frutti, which helped promote the careers of Emma Thompson, Robbie Coltrane, Maurice Roeves, and Richard Wilson, while Kenny was a much-loved actor and theatre director, spending ten years at the Lyceum Theatre in Edinburgh. He also played the skipper in Local Hero, one of my favourite films. And, of course, he was one half of the postcard exchange tradition with Bill [ibid] which was noted earlier. That brings us to Bill himself. Bill Paterson, hugely successful actor in many films such as Outlander, is not only one of The Gallant Thirty Twa, but he is also a celebrity in his own right as has been noted by Susan B[19], who met him recently when he came to lend his support to the Town Hall Restoration Project, as well as others who merely recorded a sighting with some pride! Before Bill ever embarked on the road to stardom, he was part of the story of visiting the Island every year with his parents, just like a great many others including myself. While not such a regular visitor now due to his busy career, his love of Millport remains just as strong and comes out frequently in his many anecdotes! He told the Scots Magazine "I still go into a 'Millport mood' every summer", an affliction borne by many.

John and Carol Barrowman were born in Glasgow and enjoyed that existence that we now see as so common---they spent their summer holidays in Millport. However, that might all have ended when the family emigrated to the US. There John embarked on a career as an author, singer, and presenter while Carole moved into academia. But they never forgot their childhoods or their vacation place and after numerous visits over the years, they decided to collaboratively write a fantasy trilogy that takes place on the Cumbraes. They have moved in a direction that others have taken too but they did it in a unique way. While many of the participants have read their works, it was Kyle[24] who had the excitement of meeting John in the Newton Bar and actually discussing the stories! The late Gordon Jackson was one of those actors who was never the box-office star of a movie but who quietly went about making the story memorable through his character, including another of my favourite films, The Great Escape. Gordon (1923 Glasgow-1990 London) made over 90 films and eight television series but still found time to have a place in Millport at Tindale in Kames Bay, which he frequently visited (Mark C[25]). And in the final Hollywood roll call; Emma Thompson, who has a place near Dunoon, and her Scottish actress mother, Phyllida Law, have been visitors to Millport as well. They were spotted on one occasion enjoying ice creams from the Ritz and thereby carrying on that Tinseltown tradition that a Golden Globe, Oscar, and BAFTA winner is entitled to do. Another celebrity put in a very unusual performance on the Island. Minia[31] remembers Anneke Rice, who hosted a show called "Challenge Anneke". In 1992, the challenge was to transform a derelict building at the WWII Hush Hush site on the west of the Island into a recreation/sports centre for a children's outdoor pursuit organization in precisely 72 hours (Donald & Jennie[11] and Mark C[ibid]). In a dramatic climax, recalled by many, 1000 cyclists arrived at the site on the deadline to celebrate mission accomplished. That equated very nicely to the 1000 cycles that are available for hire in the various shops in Millport! And finally, we must pay tribute to the many now unknown artists and entertainers who each summer joined Leslie's Entertainers and put on outdoor variety shows at various temporary locations in Millport, including on the grass area beside the Crosshouse and on the slope where the new church has now been placed. Some of the more senior participants, including Jennie of Donald & Jennie[11] remember these variety shows, which probably included singers in striped blazers and boaters and long-legged dancers like the shows of that era in many of the coastal resorts. Peter[12] knew the sloped facility as "The Entertainers' Pavilion" and it consisted of a wooden, tin-roofed stage affair. When it rained, as it sometimes did, the rain drumming on the roof had a tendency to drown out the entertainers on stage! Alas, they must have disappeared sometime in the 1950s.

Football has always been the number one sport in Scotland and back in the day the season only lasted for about nine months so there was time for a summer break for players, officials, and journalists alike. That permitted many to form a lasting association with Millport. For some reason, I gathered several recollections of Rangers players being regular visitors during their playing days. I did not learn of a single Celtic player. Perhaps Great Cumbrae is Protestant and Little Cumbrae is Catholic like the Todday islands in Compton MacKenzie's books? In any case, Wilson[8] and Amanda[21] remembered Bobby Shearer; Wilson[ibid] also recalled Willie Hastie while Sandra[10] noted Eric Caldow and George Young. Both Wilson[ibid] and Sandra[ibid] remembered Johnny Little whose father owned a shoe shop in Millport. That is not a bad line-up for a Millport v The Visitors game but more of that later. Wilson[ibid] also remembered Bert Comer who played for a long time for Queens Park, just in case you thought this was total blue conspiracy! Eric[3] mentioned that Wilson Humphreys, the then manager of Motherwell, and the Reverend James Martin, 65 years a minister and chaplain to the club, were also visitors to the Island.

Off the field was also represented. Archie McPherson, long-time football commentator and presenter, is fond of golf and playing regularly on the course at Millport. Fraser[32] was paired with him in one of the many holiday competitions and they had wonderful round of golf enhanced by stimulating conversation---not about golf but football! Continuing with the small ball, Sir Nick Faldo agreed to attend a charity event associated with the centenary of the Millport Golf Club. He arrived in grand style having driven his own Bentley and proceeded to conduct a very well received children's clinic before playing a full round with three honoured members. As many as 200 spectators followed play around the course and had a strenuous hike into the bargain! (Fraser[ibid])

Lastly, I picked up two more sports-related stories from my discussions. John[6] could not recall seeing any celebrities in the flesh, but he did recall seeing eleven Scottish football players in the 1974 World Cup. In the absence of a television set in the premises he was renting, he joined many others watching the games on a set

51

strategically located in a garden shed in Mount Stuart Street. And just for a nominal fee. Alas, Scotland were soon on their way home from Germany, albeit undefeated. Now if only Billy Bremner had been sharper! Chic Young is a prominent football commentator and journalist in Glasgow. He is also a frequent visitor to the Island as he is a keen boater (Susan A[4] and Liz[14]). According to Alison R[7], he likes nothing better than a round of golf followed by refreshments in the Tavern afterwards. Having his own boat, I suppose he is not at the mercy of the last ferry deadline. Suki[23] tells an amusing tale of when she was visiting with a friend and staying at the Royal George Hotel. The friend was for an early night, but Suki decided to go out on the town and ended up in the Tavern near closing time. However, after closing time passed, the doors were merely locked, and those and such as those, including the narrator, were locked in to continue the party. After a stimulating conversation with a lone male beside her at the bar, Suki just had to call and wake her friend: "You'll never guess what is happening to me. I am locked in the Tavern, and I am having great time with Chic Murray". After a long silence came the reply: "You canny be. Chic Murray is lang since deid!" It was Chic Young, and he was one of those and such as those! Music has always been a major part of the entertainment scene in Millport and live music at that, which is important. In addition, music performers, even when not playing here live, have often found excuses to visit and just hang out. I learned all sorts of stories in my discussions that were new to me. I had always believed that Arran, and Brodick in particular, were the hotbeds of music, but Millport is not far behind! But first, let's look at the music venues. The Cumbrae Club has already been mentioned and it seemed to always feature live music from a resident combo who might have lived in town. The rather grand sounding Garrison Ballroom was actually one of the rather elderly huts that probably date from WWII, or the days of the TB isolation wards. It generated differing emotions and memories. All agreed that it was the centre of entertainment, and so ideally located for a quick pass-out to Andy's Snack Bar if sustenance were desired. However, Seona & Gordon[5] enthused about the live acts like Blondie and the Searchers, while Alison R[7], Wilson[8] and Susan B[19] were insistent that only disco music was provided, not live bands. Furthermore, Jennie of Donald & Jennie[11] reminisced about old-time ballroom dancing being the featured activity. I suspect that in their own way they were all correct, it was just that the memories related to different times. The Town Hall was another music venue. It was actually a multi-purpose building housing the local cinema which could be converted into an auditorium as well as the burgh council chambers and various other public offices. It appears that both concerts and dances took place from time to time in the Town Hall and perhaps even discos. As usual the memories were a little clouded, just like those who claimed to be at Woodstock! The aforementioned Searchers might have played their gig here rather than in the Ballroom and some say they also played a gig of sorts at the Westbourne Hotel where they were lodging. That might have been a late-night jam session. Folks were there but can scarcely remember. Maybe Mike Pender remembers! The Westbourne was a thriving hotel and bar in the '70s and '80s and hosted live music acts and discos (Wilson[8]). To this day, the Royal George Hotel (now known as the Millport Pier Hotel), the Tavern bar, and the Newton lounge (at one time known as Typically Tropical as recalled by Alison R[7]) all offer live music featuring bands from around Ayrshire and Glasgow and local island talent, of which there has been a fair number over the years. Amanda[21] and Suki[23] both expressed the opinion that the quality of acts that have always come to the Island has been high. The Mansewood Hotel is now no more, the building having been converted into a care centre, but Seona & Gordon[5] remember it as the hotspot on Millport weekends with singing competitions being especially popular. Seona[ibid] told me with some pride, I think, that her mother had won the "Worst Singer" competition and was given a medal to recognize the fact!

One thing for sure is that the discos, wherever they took place, made a lasting impression on just about everyone I spoke with. I wonder how many couples met for the first time at these events. I know of a few, and they certainly have good reason to remember them! As Wilson[8] reminisced, there was nothing better than the last dance. And there was no more appropriate last song than "Please Stay" by the Cryan Shames. What an opportunity for a smooch and to whisper in her ear..." If I got down on my knee and I pleaded...."!

Special events in Millport have often been built around music, thereby contributing to the feeling that there is music to be had every weekend over the season. The biggest of all is the Country Music

Festival, now about 25 years old and featuring big-name acts from the US and the UK playing on multiple stages contained within large marquees. On that weekend the population of Millport swells to its highest with most people donning western attire and many of the local businesses achieving an instant conversion to a western theme. There are probably more American and Confederate flags flying on the Island that weekend than there are in the rest of the UK if not Europe, although the latter flag has come under fire recently in a wave of PC consciousness. The official festival also has a fringe festival, just like its big brother in Edinburgh, which means that every conceivable venue in the town is hopping with local talent and splinter acts from the official festival once their gig there has been completed. Without a doubt the Country Music Festival is a big deal for Millport as noted by Alison R[7] and many of the other participants. However, this is one area in particular where the opinions of the permanent residents might significantly differ from those of the visitors, and it would be interesting to make a comparison. Josh[17], our participant from Texas, had perhaps the fondest memories of the event. No surprise there, considering he performed in it one year under the moniker of Kid Millport. He loved the atmosphere, the quality of the performers, and the fact the island was completely given over to the event for that entire weekend. He would love to return some day with his band, which is now getting well established around Houston, Texas. There are also other events like Happy Daze, with topnotch tribute bands and local talent; the Scooter Rally, when hundreds of mods descend on the island on their scooters for a weekend of preening and music, enough to warm the hearts of Pete Townsend and the late Ronnie Lane no end. Furthermore, there is the September Weekend, the traditional closure of the holiday season. It is all great fun!

Among the many music acts that have played on the Island or just come to hang out are Tony West, Jim Diamond, Gaberlunzie, Christian/Chris McClure Section, Andy Stewart, Kenneth McKellar, Sydney Devine, Love and Money, James Grant, Primal Scream, Shane Richie, Billy Connolly, Agatha's Moment, Middle of the Road (Cumbrae Club), Salvation with Midge Ure, Poets (Garrison Ballroom), Harmony Grass, Billy and the 4 Just Men, Beatstalkers, Pathfinders, Dean Ford & The Gaylords (later Marmalade), Big 3, Beings, early Pink Floyd (only rumoured alas) and David McNevin (of Bread Love and Dreams) to mention just a few in no particular order. Seona & Gordon[5] recall Tony West, after his success on Opportunity Knocks, singing in both the Newton and Tavern. Wilson[8] remembers Jim Diamond performing and at other times just hanging out in Millport before he made it big in London. Andy Stewart was a very big star, mainly in the '60s when he had several world-wide hits centring on Scottish tradition. Clad in his omnipresent kilt, he took his song "A Scottish Soldier" into the UK charts for 36 weeks, to number one in most Commonwealth countries, and even to number 69 in the US charts. He also owned a house in Kames Bay and was a frequent visitor to the Island when his busy schedule permitted. I remember seeing him striding along the promenade in his holiday civvies. Perhaps it was the absence of the kilt, but I could not get over how small he was, he had always stood so tall when he was belting out the ballads! Every one of the participants remembered Andy Stewart, just like they did Duncan Macrae and Kathie Kay, but Sandra[10] had one unusual recollection. Andy was advertising for a nanny for his considerable brood of young children. She applied and was called for an interview. However, when she met the children and learned that she would be required to wear a somewhat ostentatious uniform, she decided to forgo the opportunity! Funnily enough, Valerie[26] had a similar recollection of those four young children so there must be something in it. I wonder what they grew up to be! Amanda[21] mentioned Sydney Devine, who was a frequent visitor who tended to be noticed. He drove a pink Cadillac! Spencer[16] encountered Andrew Inness of Primal Scream on a daytrip to Millport. They discovered that they knew each other from childhood Boys' Brigade days when both had been pipers. Spencer[ibid] reported that Andrew was more interested in talking about piping than his own career and was particularly interested in how he could acquire a home on the Island just like Spencer! Shane Richie, soap star and successful country singer, was headliner at a recent Country Music Festival and made a big impression on stage and around the town (Josh[17] and Amanda[21]). An even bigger star, Billy Connolly, had a fondness for Millport in addition to Arran and Rothesay. Bill[18] got to know Billy well in Glasgow and they were both aware of the other's love for Millport, but they never met there because they traditionally visited in different months. That was something that tended to happen with most visitors, the consistency of their scheduled visits. I was one of the exceptions;

we travelled whenever my dad could arrange some time off work. Mark K[20] remembers meeting Billy Connolly in the Newton, which was known to be one of his hangouts. The nature of the encounter? Billy scrounging a light for his fag. You remember those days! Lastly, David McNiven from Denniston, Glasgow was the founder of Bread Love & Dreams in Edinburgh in the '70s. The band was similar to the Incredible String Band without attaining the same success but many, including my good self, preferred them thanks to their three albums. Bill[18] also came from Denniston but never ever ran into David there. However, for a number of summers they holidayed in Millport on the same fortnight and immediately hit it off. So much so, that they took to busking on the promenade with David performing his own folk songs and Bill reciting Shakespeare! Only in Millport, you say! Bill[ibid] remembers one fine night in the bar of McGillivray Arms Hotel (now sadly no more) when David commandeered the honky-tonk piano and together with friends (all underage by the way) gave an impromptu performance to great acclaim. While Millport will always undergo gradual change, it is hoped that it never loses its musical traditions. They are very much the heartbeat of the place.

We close this chapter of celebrities and places of entertainment in the world of the thespian. The Town Hall, at the time of writing undergoing an exciting transformation and renaissance, served as the cinema for many years. There were a great many reminiscences of spending wet days at the "picter-hoose" and especially going to the horror shows that I think came on at about 11pm. That meant by the time the show ended all the lights on the Island had been shut off and the overwhelming darkness mixed well with recent memories of Dracula and Frankenstein. I know I covered the half mile from the Town Hall to West Bay in near Olympic time. Seona & Gordon[5] gleefully remember a brother who decided he was not enjoying the film and left just before midnight. Unfortunately, before he could make it home, he was plunged into darkness, all alone, well except for Dracula and Frankenstein! Children could always be cruel to one another! Anne & Ian[9] painfully remembered that half of the seating was the regular if old cinema variety while the other half was long wooden benches. I seem to remember people (not me of course) paying for the cheap seats and then sneaking up to the softish ones once the lights went down! In any case, it was great day's or night's entertainment precisely because it was happening in Millport. Never mind that the cinema did not compare to those fancy ones at home. Sandra[10] remembered the distinctly low-tech projection equipment frequently breaking down amid a chorus of slow handclaps. Now, you did not get that in every cinema. Apparently, when the Town Hall was being renovated recently, the projector and some reels of film were unearthed. What a tale they could tell. I hope they are preserved, just for posterity! When the Town Hall was closed down for a number of years, Millport lost its cinema like so many other small towns in Scotland. However, a great innovation emerged thanks to government and sponsorship money---The Screen Machine, a trailer that opens up to reveal an 80-seat, air-conditioned, mobile digital cinema. The Screen Machine routinely visits a number of islands to provide the latest in theatre entertainment. It is one of the very few examples where the islanders have an advantage over the mainlanders! I recall one of my attendances with great fondness. The cinema was parked as usual on the Old Pier. But it was a stormy night and the trailer seemed to be bouncing up and down even as we entered it. Then to add to the drama what was playing but Mama Mia! Pretty soon, 80 Millportonians and visitors were up strutting their stuff and just adding to the feeling of a bouncy castle. Were we ever in any danger of ending up in the Clyde? I doubt it but it sure was fun. I wonder what Abba would have made of it!

Finally, if Hollywood is a little too rich for your digestion, there is always the local dramatic society and the shows they put on in the Garrison hut next to the hut that used to be the grand ballroom! Minia[31] and others mentioned with great sentimentality the entertaining shows. There is nothing better than seeing the local butcher or hairdresser in a completely different context, acting for all they are worth in a dramatic or comedic fashion as the part demands. Or sometimes, the part does not demand it, but you get it anyway and the whole audience laps it up!

Chapter 7

Bicycles Galore

IX One or two bicycles about to set off from Mapes.

Is Cumbrae the bicycle capital of the world? I have always thought so. It definitely feels like it when I sit on my porch on the west side of the Island at about two o'clock in the afternoon and all the day trippers have arrived and have been suitably equipped at one of the cycle hire shops. They wobble past me, say hello to the cows in the field on the other side of the road and then turn to me and make a very consistent comment about being ready for a glass of that wine that I am enjoying! But is it really the capital? I suppose things have to be looked at in context. For example, there are estimated to be more than 500 million bicycles in China among a population of 1.3 billion, making a coverage of 37%, while in the Netherlands there are 16.5 million bicycles among a population of 16.6 million, making a coverage of 99%. On Cumbrae there are more than 1000 bikes for hire plus say 100 resident bikes for a population of 1,300. OK OK! A wee bit of a distortion. That's what statistics are all about, is it not! Suffice it to say that it feels like there are a lot of bicycles on the Island.

The participants, to a person, had things to say about their experiences on bikes. Most of them, in fact, mentioned that they did not possess a bike at home, probably understandable if they resided in the centre of a city, but they associated their visit to Cumbrae with being attached to a bike for their entire stay. Alison R[7], Wilson[8], Eileen[13], and Fraser[32] all noted a trip to the hire shop was the very first thing to do when they arrived in Millport, before even the ubiquitous trunks were opened. And they also mentioned that a hire was arranged for the entire duration of the stay. Hiring rates have always seemed to be extremely reasonable (easy for me to say, I was not paying in the early days), even to this day, and there is a significant saving in hiring over a longer period than a single or half day. This put the old two-week and four-week visitors at an advantage over the day trippers and I saw some sort of moral justification in this. After all, we were closer to residents than those who just popped over for the day! I am sure today there are many more day hires than longer hires and that is just how things have evolved. I have to admit that I see it as the right of every child to be mounted on a bicycle to enjoy the full experience of a visit to the Island---and the faces of so many that pass by suggest they agree with me.

The joy of cycling on that almost completely flat island was not the sole right of children, however. Participants reported that their entire family climbed on bicycles (John[6], Eileen[13], Valerie[26], and Christine[30]). That is precisely why, to this day, when you have the misfortune or make the ill-advised decision to take your car around the island, or even along the promenade road, you will frequently be brought to a standstill by a group of ten or even twenty bikes slowly and erratically making their way along, at their pace. For there is an unwritten rule on the

Island…bicycles take priority, everywhere! That can make it tricky for car drivers and it is exacerbated by the varying qualities of ridership exhibited by a lot in the saddle. As if to underscore the point, Valerie[ibid] remembers as one of a group of children cycling with gay abandon on Stuart Street and being warned of the impending arrival of a car, that she uttered the immortal words: "Well, it will just have to drive around us!". Many of the participants remembered that they first learned to ride a bike on the Island, and some passed on the skill to their children in turn (Sandra[10], Susan B[19], Mark K[20], Christine[30], and Fraser[32]). And it was Eileen[13] who made the profound observation that it was the lack of cars back in the day that it made it such an appropriate location to make those first wobbly attempts at proficiency. Alas, today the road is far too crowded with cars and day trippers who appear to be cycling for the very first time, judging by the wobbles. And I do not just mean children! Finally, Clare[22] and family are frequent visitors to their place on the Island and are all keen cyclists. How have they adapted to the change with more cars and more day tripper cyclists? Simply. "We cycle in the evening once all the day trippers have disappeared for the day!" The perception of safety in cycling on the island is interesting, however. While most, including Mary[1], Eileen[13], and Evelyn[29], would hark back to the good old days when cars were few and bicycles reigned supreme, there does remain the conviction that there are few better or safer places on Earth to get on a bike.

When circumnavigation of the Island is contemplated and that must apply to 95% of those who have hired a bike, the great debate is whether to go clockwise or anti-clockwise. Does it matter? It seems to. If clockwise, one will reach Fintry Bay sooner and that bodes well for an ice cream or drink. If anti-clockwise, there used to be a similar opportunity at Fairhaven but that is no longer in operation. Never fear, Fintry will roll around eventually. Now, you might think I am making too much of this debate, but I assure you the participants held very strong views and were never inclined to vary their choice. Seona & Gordon[5] and Christine were avowed anti-clockwisers because they had interest in the Queen Victoria Profile, Marine Biological Station, wishing well and Fairhaven café and all would be reached earlier by their chosen route, while Clare[22] always went the opposite way in order to hit Fintry earlier. All very sound logical answers to the debate but consider the funny story Scott Ferris of the famous Mapes Hire Shop told me. When asked by a nervous day tripper, who had just hired her first bicycle, as to which way she should go, he answered that it mattered not because either way would bring her back to the shop, the island being tantamount to a circle. She headed off a little uncertainly. When she finally returned to the shop a lot later than she had indicated at the outset, she confessed that she must have missed the shop at the end of her first circumnavigation and had ended up going around the Island twice!

Once the trips around the perimeter road, (the road being constructed in 1875 by the way), have been completed to everyone's satisfaction, there are three internal roads on offer. The internal road from Kames Bay to the perimeter road almost at Cumbrae Slip is a shorter means to get to the ferry now from the town. Hence it is heavily favoured by cars. It is not the safest option for cyclists, and it involves a fairly steep climb offset by a nice freewheel down the other side of the hill. It is not greatly used by cyclists. There is also a straight hill climb from the Old Pier all the way to the Golf Club, passing the Kirkton Caravan Site on the way. Other than by people staying in the caravans, this road is not much used by cyclists either because it is too steep plus you don't often see golfers with their bag of clubs on their backs pedalling away like stink in order to make their tee-time! Having said all that, Amanda[21] has the fondest memories of freewheeling down the hill and hoping to make a stop before disappearing off the pier! She never mentioned how she felt about the need to pedal back up the hill to the caravan site. The final internal road is the most interesting of the three, being a circular road from the town at the Garrison that leads to the highest point of the island, the Glaidstone, and back to the town at Kames Bay. While the views from there are quite amazing on a clear day and intriguing even on a cloudy day, getting there is quite a challenge for most cyclists, excepting those characters that wear the tight vests and shorts and funny hats and probably wish the incline was steeper. For the other cyclists, it is an achievement to make the top, which is rewarded with the virtual freewheel down the other side of the circular road. Memories among The Gallant Thirty Twa understandably varied, with Josh[17] proud that he was able to take his achievement back to the USA, perhaps to share it while on stage performing, while John[6] professed that the family were all avid cyclists on the Island but steered away from any assault on the Glaidstone! I have achieved the climb a few times but not recently I have to add. That feeling of having rubber legs at the summit tends to spoil the enjoyment of the view!

In general terms, hired bikes can be used to explore every inch of the Island if one has sufficient energy and occasional ingenuity. But, as Mary[1] and every one of the hire shops staff will remind you: "Don't take the bike on the beach!" In fact, Frank Mapes Sr of the eponymous shop was known to be a good deal more emphatic at the beginning of the hire and an even greater deal more emphatic should an infraction have been revealed at its end!

It seems the Island will always be synonymous with bikes, but the types of bikes have changed over the years, adding to the glamour of the spectacle. Tandems are much more common now, as Tracy[15] noted. However, the technique of propelling them seems unchanged with the driver doing most of the work while the rider behind can take a break when they feel like it by lifting their feet off the pedals. It also seems still to be the tradition that man sits up front while woman rides behind but that may be an issue of control (what kind of control you may ask) more than anything else. A passing tandem is very often accompanied by hoots of laughter amid the firm conviction that they would not be doing this on Sauchiehall Street or Princes Street. In recent years, multiple rider contraptions have emerged to accommodate as many as ten pedallers, all facing each other. To everyone's amazement, the bike actually moves in one direction and hopefully the desired one. These bikes are often seen in other parts of the world and sometimes take on the role of mobile drinking vehicles with large ice buckets containing beers and wines in the centre and within reach of all the riders. I don't think these vehicles have made a debut on the Island---just yet! And finally, in spite of the fact that I have emphasized time and time again that the Island is extremely flat with only one hill, and even it can be avoided, and a couple of gentle slopes, the bicycle revolution has hit Cumbrae with the arrival of the e-bike. Electrically assisted bikes come in various shapes and forms and seem to get more and more sophisticated with each season. Alison[7], Susan[19], and Suki[23] were among many to extol the virtues of the e-bike with Alison claiming that she was now able to easily climb the hill into Fintry Bay. If the gentle incline there qualifies as a hill, I am a Dutchman! However, having said that, I have to confess that I am the proud owner of an e-bike and there is nothing finer than to feel the wind in your hair as you whizz along!!

Not all visitors hired bikes. A fair number of our participants brought their own, either on a per trip basis or they were able to leave them in readiness for the next visit. As cars and those humungous motor homes grew in popularity, so too did the practice of bringing bikes over from the mainland. In fact, the latter seem capable of transporting a whole fleet of bikes precariously tied on at the rear or on the roof. But even in the days gone-by when travel was by train, personal bikes were often placed in the guard's van at the rear where the trunks were located. Liz[14] and Valerie[26] fondly remembered having their own bikes with them on the Island. Amanda[21] remembered that she only possessed one bike and it permanently resided in Millport while Christine[30] did something similar by bringing her brand-new Christmas present to Millport in 1954 and leaving it there for frequent use. Among the more thoughtful, or perhaps it was more wealthy cyclists, Kyle[24] kept two bikes here---one of the racing variety, the other a mountain bike, their uses to be dictated by the terrain---, while Fraser[32] also maintains two ---one regular and one electric, their uses to be dictated by the prevailing condition of his knees!

As we close this homage to the two wheels (although in some cases it can be three or four or more!) and their love affair with Cumbrae, it is only right to pay tribute to the bicycle hire shops on the Island, surely an essential and hopefully forever thriving service if ever there was one. It appears that prior to WWII there was one bicycle hirer in Millport. Jennie of Donald & Jennie[11] recalls Morrison's Garage, which is probably on the same site as the current RK Horn Garage, as the go-to place. There may have been earlier shops, but they did not come up in my conversations. Since WWII, there have been four shops strategically placed along the promenade, or just off it, throughout the town. Three of the shops have existed through the different tourism eras, starting with the mix of two and four-week visitors and day trippers and evolving into a far greater percentage of day trippers. During the earlier era, it is very noticeable that visitors identified a favoured shop, probably in many cases aligned to the proximity of where they stayed, and remained tremendously loyal to that shop, even to this day. Returning day trippers may have also formed a close association with a particular shop but in the present day, with a huge upswell of new trippers, the choice of shop has probably been more random and might depend on advertising or where they alighted from the bus or even the respective lengths of the queues outside the shops. Perhaps as a consequence of this new trend in selection, the town has lost two of its cycle-hire shops. Both those shops could be described as having the inferior location relative to the other two. And yet, demand for hires has remained high. Mapes opened in 1948 close to the centre of the promenade and has been dressed in striking red for most, if not all, of those years. Mapes is an icon, not just as the major cycle hirer but also as an amazing traditional toyshop that every child of today and every adult who was once a child will gravitate towards in wonderment! Run by generations of the Mapes family until recently, it is now run by Scott and Deborah Ferris who seem to have hit on edging a perfect business model into an even more perfect business model. Seldom can a business transition have worked so well. More than half the participants named the shop as their favourite and virtually everyone thought highly of it. Mary[1] could never get over the little child seats attached to the rear of the bike (and now superseded by child and pet carriers towed behind the bike) that were a Millport staple that she never saw anywhere else. Alison[7], Donald & Jennie[11], Eileen[13], and Bill[18] all remembered Frank Mapes Sr, the founder of the shop, who relished having the reputation of being a curmudgeon not to be messed with if one did not offer his cycles absolute respect but otherwise was just a pussy cat. Bill[ibid] made reference to Frank's 11th Commandment, "Thou shall not take the bike near the beach!" that has remained with him to this day. And Tracy[15], along with many others, spoke very highly of the new ownership that bodes well for the continued dominance of cycles on the Island. The second shop, Rafferty Cycles, was located on Mount Stuart Street and therefore became the favourite of the Kames Bay set in particular. The building was not much to look at and had previously been a byre, where Peter[12] recalled a Mrs Cunningham hand-milking her several cows twice per day! In later years Sandy Morton took over and renamed the business Mortons Cycles. Again, this transition was achieved without a hiccup in service or any reduction in affection felt by the customers. The shop under both owners also offered a television hire and repair service and later a computer repair service that many of the participants (including Susan A[4] and Wilson[8]) remembered and appreciated. Sadly, with Sandy's retirement and ultimate passing, there was no-one to take over and the business was lost. Many participants mentioned the fairness of the cycle hire rates with big discounts on longer terms and the practice of giving small children a tricycle at no charge.

The third shop was Bremners on Cardiff Street. It had a very loyal clientele as well, notably those staying in the nearby West Bay, myself included. Sadly, the shop has recently been sold and the premises repurposed. Lastly, On Your Bike is a relative newcomer to the cycle hire business, being located in a prime position next door to the Ritz Café. It does not have the history to feature so strongly in the memories I gathered, but it attracts a good many of those first-time day trippers because not only does it offer a full range of all types of cycles, it has been at the forefront of the e-bike revolution and diversified into offering all kinds of simple watercrafts to be launched in the harbour. This has proved to be a welcome successor to the small rowing boats and motorboats that were for hire from Newton Beach by as many as four companies in the heydays of the '50s through to the '80s. Many of the participants spoke longingly of the boat hires and Fraser[32] recalled the apparent rivalry among the operators that tended to prompt a particular loyalty to one. If you were a Hunter person, you would not be seen dead in a Mauchline craft!

It is safe to say that the glorious history of the bicycle on Cumbrae is likely to continue to thrive thanks to dedication and innovation of the shops that service this important part of the island culture. While recreational trends can come and go across society, if anything the humble and now not so humble bicycle seem destined to thrive and to enjoy a special place here.

Chapter 8

The Garrison and The Cathedral

X Iconic buildings, the Garrison House and the Cathedral of the Isles.

There are two iconic buildings in Millport, three if one includes the Town Hall which at the time of writing is undergoing an exciting restoration that hopefully will see it ultimately return to the prominence it enjoyed in its halcyon days. These are The Garrison House and Grounds and The Cathedral of the Isles. Each has a fascinating history and has enjoyed its own evolution connected to but in other ways independent of the development of the town of Millport. And each seems to have played a very different part in the memories of the participants I have spoken with. In Scotland, as well as in the other parts of the United Kingdom, towns of even modest size often have castles or mansion houses and churches of all denominations. However, there are few towns that are as small as Millport that have one of each in magnificent design and condition as Millport does. That condition was not always so but more of that later, and the town of Millport could very easily be the city of Millport, in spite of its limited population, but again more of that later.

The Garrison House is a magnificent building sitting in walled grounds of about 1.2 hectares or 3 acres in old money, on the waterfront of the town with an unencumbered view of Millport Bay and the two Eileans. The house was built in 1745 to specifically provide appropriate status accommodation for the captain and senior officers of the revenue cutter Royal George. In that time of lucrative, contracted-out customs and excise services on behalf of the Crown, even the lower ranks of the cutter were able to construct modest mansions, mainly on Bute Terrace, with even more imposing views over the bay toward the mainland. In the early part of the 19th century, the house was acquired by the 4th Earl of Glasgow, and he set about extensive remodelling and extension to the gothic battlement architecture; in other words, it became almost a castle. The good lord also constructed the first pier in the town in 1833 and thereby opened up Millport to the burgeoning steamship business then exploding on the Clyde. In the late 1800s, the Marquess of Bute, the other major landowner on Cumbrae and places well beyond, became the owner of the Garrison after Lord Glasgow suffered financial disaster. In 1908, he commissioned further extensive remodelling of the house and the development of the sunken gardens to the front to create the exterior image that largely exists to this day. In 1948, the house was leased in order to accommodate county council offices and it existed as that until 1997 when reorganization of local councils in Scotland caused the presence to largely disappear on the Island. The once majestic building then passed into a period of rapid neglect and decay and by time of the entry into the new millennium it was in such a state of disrepair that there were many advocating for its demolition. In 2001, the matter

67

seemed to have been taken out of the hands of the planners or plotters when a crippling fire all but destroyed the house, including the loss of the roof and the interior floors. Many of the participants I Interviewed were aware of the fire and the perhaps inevitable speculation of arson, but I could not elicit a definitive story from them on the latter. However, this was going to be one example where recourse to permanent island residents was going to help in the production of this book. After speaking with authoritative voices in the town, I am satisfied that the true story of the fire centres around misadventure and with absence of malice. It was an accident that could have been avoided but it was not deliberate! In an ironic way, the fire did lead to a happy ending because while the call for demolition of the now eyesore became even stronger, there also emerged a community call for "Save the Garrison" and the creation of the Cumbrae Community Development Company. The action group did sterling work and over an agonizingly long time it managed to acquire the funds and the specialist expertise to fully restore the building to its original glory including converting the interior for important local community uses. In 2008 and at a cost of £5 million, the Garrison House reopened to great acclaim and now features the island medical centre, library, museum, café, council administrative offices, art gallery, craft shop, model schoolhouse (alas now closed) and community meeting rooms. If ever £5 million was well spent, it was here and if ever there was a case for a National Lottery, it was here! The Garrison quickly became the focal point of the town and hence the island in a strong manner, perhaps even more so than it had previously been.

In the period before the fire, the participants had abundant memories of the Garrison grounds, as we will learn, but they did not have strong recollections of the interior of the house. I suppose the county administrative offices were there if one wanted to conduct business, but few visitors had reason to do so. There were two very contrasting eating places therein---a very formal tea-room with white starched tablecloths and silver cutlery and a pseudo-American snack bar. Few said much about the former although John[6] and Wilson[8] 'fessed up to having at least been in it, but Bill[18] said his family avoided it for being too "sedate". Other than the coffee crowd in the mornings, I wonder what kind of clientele it had. I vaguely remember it as a stuffy-looking place and not one my family would go into. Fraser[32] remembered his multi-families group assembling in the Garrison every morning to plan out the rest of the day (as if it needed planning); then men and boys would make for the golf course while women and girls would retire to the tea-room, but for coffee. Presumably that was the holiday treat; otherwise, it might have been for tea. The other restaurant was the centre of Millport, if not the entire universe, a real happening place---variously called Andy's Snack Bar or the Beachcomber. It was your stereotypical American hangout joint, except this was not America. Andy and Martha, the owners and servers, were the coolest couple, Andy even looked like he was American, Bill[18] recalled. And they offered the biggest jukebox with the best selection of current hits, although other cafés were quick to learn what the young people wanted and followed suit. Coke floats, burgers with lashings of onions, espresso coffees from a wheezing contraption that threated to explode at the climax of its cycle, and high stools that one could perilously rock onto two legs, just for the joy of living dangerously! Oh, the joy of that place. Holiday romances blossomed there. Bill[18] described it as a "honey pot" that just attracted young people. And in that wonderfully innocent way of those times (Seona & Gordon[5], Alison[7], and Mark[20]), you almost expected Cliff Richard to pop out from behind the jukebox and sing "The Young Ones" or "Summer Holiday". Either would have worked. I was only ever in the place when I was taken there. I was too young to venture in on my own. Fraser[32] also remembers being in the same situation, but it was just enough to stand outside and listen to the juke box and the laughter emitting from within. Other favourites that participants longingly recalled in the Beachcomber were Zoom ice-lollies (Eric[3]) and Knickerbocker Glories (how American that sounds) and double nougat wafers (Eileen[13]). Eileen and I had a cautious giggle when I revealed that a double nougat wafer ice cream was in those days known as a black man where I came from in Edinburgh. I wonder if it is still known as a double nougat wafer. We already know the answer to the other! The final feature of the Garrison House that people remembered from before the fire was the library, which was much more modest than the modern facility of today with its computer lab and all sorts of media for loan. Then it was just a few books and nothing more. Both Sandra[10] and Donald & Jennie[11] remembered taking out books for those exceptionally rare wet days but also recalled that there was a shop on the front that rented out books for a modest sum and it had a far better selection!

The grounds of the Garrison have been the epicentre for a lot of activities associated with Millport over the years and were lovingly recalled by The Gallant Thirty Twa. In fact, there have been an amazing array of activities in what seems like constant change from the 1950s to the present day. As Millport has always been about family fun, the activities have been tailor-made to meet those needs and have lodged in people's memories for most of their lives. Top of the list was the funfair, vividly recalled by Mary[1], Wilson[8], Alison B[27], and Moira[28], or simply 'the shows" as named by Seona & Gordon[5] and Spencer[16]. There has been a funfair in existence to this day and it conjures up all sorts of memories. Mary[ibid] rattled off flying helicopters, roundabouts, flashing lights and pulsating music (that sought to compete with Beachcomber jukebox) and that just sums things up perfectly. Today there is a much more refined air about the funfair, whether it be the part remaining within the Garrison Grounds or the other part located with the Crazy Golf on the promenade. What does that say about the society of today? The trampolines have gradually moved from their original location in the grounds to the promenade but remain very popular. Mary[ibid], Susan M[4], Alison R[7], Liz[14], Susan B[19], and Amanda[21] all spoke fondly of the ups and downs of their experience and only the latter opined that she preferred the old location within the grounds.

We pass now to pools and ponds, all much enjoyed in their time but now removed from the Garrison Grounds. The paddling pool, or wading pool for North American readers, was extremely popular in its day. I remember it being so busy it was more a of a standing still pool as opposed to a wading pool! Incidentally, there were two boating ponds in town too, one in Kames Bay and the other in West Bay. These were not intended to be wading pools; they were for toy yachts and motorboats. Moira[28] recalled her father organizing yacht races for children who were known to him, and anyone else that happened to show up. However, when the wind did not blow or the batteries ran out and the boats had to be rescued, someone, often dad, had to be sent in and they became wading pools (Spencer[16])! Back to the Garrison paddling pool. There were lots of pleasant memories from Mary[1], Seona & Gordon[5], Alison R[7], Donald & Jennie[11], Susan B[19], and Alison

B[27]. However, I was the only one who seemed to remember that the water was never very clean. Who knows what was deposited in it and perhaps it is better not to know? Perhaps coming from the more genteel side of Scotland, I was more sensitive to those issues. In any case, everyone loved it, even Lorraine[2] who fell in and required stitches. She did not mention a tetanus jab, but I would have recommended it! Now the burning question---why was the pool removed when it was obviously so very popular? We will get back to that. There was another pool of sorts in the grounds too although I have little memory of it. Apparently, there was a duck pond and lily pond or probably one serving the two purposes. Seona & Gordon[5] remembered it well, Donald & Jennie[11] did too. They were amazed at the variety of ducks that called it home. However, the lasting memory for Anne of Anne & Ian[9] was the frequent infusion of Fairy Liquid into the pond by person or persons unknown. I doubt the ducks were amused but was that the reason for the pond's removal? We have to remember that this was the time when the UK was coming totally under the influence of Brussels law makers. Hmmm!

Putting was always a popular activity in Millport. At one time there were three splendid courses at the Bowling Club, Kames Bay and the Garrison Grounds. I played them all frequently and I could even play on my own. I kept scores and checked if I had improved on yesterday's efforts. It was a big competition in my mind. It was just a pity there was not a fourth course or else I could well have been competing in the four majors---well before Tiger Woods! Alas, now there is but one course at the Bowling Club and it is not overused. I wonder why that is. Do kids not play with imagination anymore? I guess the chip in the computer game provides the imagination for free. The Garrison course was always a bit cramped but still a pleasure to play. Eric[3], Seona & Gordon[5], Donald & Jennie[11], Clare[22], and Fraser[32] might well have been competing in my imaginary tournaments for they all remember playing there too. Now here is a funny thing. Around about the same time as we are just talking about, there was also a pitch and putt course within the Garrison grounds that I knew absolutely nothing about. In fact, I only learned about it a couple of years ago. That would been my fourth required major course at a stretch, but I never knew. I was never told. Who can I blame for that? Wilson[8] and Donald & Jennie[ibid] knew all about it and played on it but told me about it when it was way too late for it too has just disappeared! That is a pity. No doubt the land has been put to alternative use. But is it better use? It seems the pitch and putt was very popular.

Now we turn to the activity in the grounds that seems to have been the most popular and the one whose disappearance has caused the most ire. Suffice it to say, I encountered what was tantamount to venom from participants when the subject was raised. I am talking about the tennis courts. I had no idea that they were held in such high esteem. I was a keen tennis player, well at least during the month after Wimbledon, but I never played on the Garrison courts. Perhaps it was because they were always too busy and therein lies the tale. Tennis always seems to have been popular in Millport. There are reported courts in Kames Bay since the 1920s but they gave way to brand new courts constructed in the Garrison Grounds in 1950. Thereafter, they were a hot-ticket item where many families spent at least a part of most days of their holiday. Nobody seem to quite remember when they disappeared, but they are not forgotten. Making reservations seems to have been a crucial first step to getting on court and was not without its difficulties. Donald and Jennie[11] recall the practice of rewarding the lady who ran the courts with a box of chocolates, but they did not reveal if it was an essential component of the booking process or just being nice. Bill[18] remembers getting around the issue by having a season ticket bought for him each year, thereby allowing him to play every day! Fraser[32] was another who immediately remembered advance booking of the court as being essential. He was just one of many to express the great shame that the courts are now no more. He remembered them as not just a great place to play but also to watch the games that were imbued with a good deal of skill. Those skills were put to the test in weekly competitions that seem to have produced fierce rivalries as remembered by Bill[18]. Liz[14], another who professed great anger with the fact that the courts have gone, had an amusing recollection of the Thursday Mixed-Doubles competitions. She and her brother were great competitors and probably would not have relished being paired together, However, they hoped for top-notch partners coming out of the draw process. As chance would have it, each week, at least in Liz's memory, she was paired with Charles from Milngavie, who was a notable player in the West of Scotland. Her brother almost always was paired with an unknown beginner. She has long wondered if the fact that Charles' mother was responsible for arranging pairs and draws had anything to do it. I threw in a posit that the same lady might well have gone on to head up the seeding system at Wimbledon! Without a doubt, of all the activities that have graced the Garrison Grounds over the years and then disappeared, tennis was the most popular. Way more than half the participants recollected playing on the courts but also expressed their displeasure that they were not available now should they wish to make a comeback. Why were they lost at their apparent peak of popularity and use? I could not get to the bottom of this one unfortunately. Some participants suggested it was a condition of getting the lottery funding to restore the house but that does not seem to make sense to me and the timing of the two events might not even align. I guess sometimes things in Millport just remain as rumours and can be added to and adjusted as time marches on.

It would be wrong to give the impression that the Garrison is all about memories and the past. It is still the very vibrant centre of Millport. Moira[28] described it as "the centre of our world", where everything happens or where plans are laid for it to happen somewhere else. Eileen[13] and Fraser[32] both recalled the daily ritual of entire families gathering in the grounds to discuss what everyone was going to do that day and, perhaps most importantly, when they would reassemble. In many cases it would be a good deal later in the day. Millport was, and to some extent still is, a place where you could dismiss the kids with an appointed time to return and not see them again until then. And all the while, never worry about them! One of the lasting activities, still a favourite with young and old today, is the model railway hut with its impressive layouts. It is maintained, indeed further developed, by enthusiastic adults masquerading as kids and is still enjoyed by all, although Eric[3] and Amanda[21] might have been the only participants to actually own up to it! That makes at least three of us. A number of The Gallant Thirty Twa reminisced about the weekly, if not daily, competitions that used to be held on the beaches, promenade, and within the Garrison Grounds. Every tourist stood a chance of winning something if they were game enough to enter and Mary[1], for one, claimed family success in the "Nobbly Knees" and "Bonnie Baby" categories! Most of these triumphs were captured by the omnipresent camera of the renowned photographer Walter Kerr, who seemed to know just when to show up for a snap. Even if not a competition winner, many families could have an impromptu portrait taken by the great man. Eileen[13], Moira[28], Evelyn[29], and Fraser[32] could all remember a family photograph being taken every year around the Garrison. Even more impressively, they could recall which drawer all the photographs were stuffed away in at home! Of course, the grounds are also the scene of those hopping music events previously discussed, being the Country Music Festival and the discos, dances, and dramas held in the DA Hall, sometimes known as the Garrison Ballroom. I will leave the last word on these activities to capture their impact to Clare[22], who stated boldly "there was nothing like it in Glasgow!". But it would be misleading to suggest that every activity in the Garrison had to be of the organized and planned variety. The grounds were a terrific place just to play simple pretend games as a child whether it being trying to leap over the gaps on the surrounding castle-like wall (Alison R[7])---there is probably a technical name for that---or gathering with the local resident kids to play hide and seek in a site that could have been deliberately designed for that very purpose (Amanda[21]).

Lastly, it is only appropriate to give credit to the previously mentioned Cumbrae Community Development Company for its sterling efforts to make the Garrison House and Grounds an ongoing, viable economic entity. It is constantly looking for opportunities and has been instrumental in recent years in the emergence of holiday apartments, the community radio station Radio Millport and its spiffy, hi-tech studio in the Garrison Lodge (where this humble scribe lives out his 1960s musical fantasies on Tuesday nights at 6pm!), and the new motorhome parking site (an admirable attempt to get those road monsters off the front street!).

The Cathedral of the Isles, physically on the other side of the same street that houses the Garrison, was conceived and constructed by George Boyle, 6th Earl of Glasgow, a staunch Episcopalian and a descendant of the Earl who was behind the development of the Garrison and the creation of the pier. It was opened in 1851 and attained full cathedral status in 1876. It is a stunning building in the Gothic Revival style where the spire reaches into the sky, and its height is more than three times the length of its base in the nave. A theological college was added to the main building and functioned as such until 1885. Thereafter, its utilization has been somewhat erratic. From 1919-

27, it accommodated nuns from the order of the Community of St Andrew (displaced from their home in Joppa then just outside Edinburgh and whose presence around the shaded grounds spawned a delicious legend that provided this scribe with the basis for a spooky short-story) From 1975-85, it hosted the visiting Community of Celebration from Texas, USA (including our participant Josh[17]), and since then has functioned as a retreat house for organized events and individuals seeking basic accommodation within a pastoral surrounding.

The Cathedral has always functioned as a place of worship. In fact, it was one of five active churches in Millport as recently as 1960. And yet until fairly recently, with the exception of those regular worshippers, it has remained somewhat aloof, place that residents and visitors knew all about but did not necessarily set foot in! Almost half the participants confessed that they had never been inside in their lives, for varying reasons, including not being able to relate to the Episcopalian religion and not wanting to waste any of their precious holiday time on religious matters. The latter position, endorsed by his father, surprised Bill[18], considering his father was a session clerk in Glasgow. Bill[ibid] described the vacation as an "agnostic holiday", a term I had not heard before, but which seems to adequately sum things up. Other observations included the feeling that the Cathedral did not encourage visitors in those days, something that has since changed significantly (Eileen[13]); it has uncomfortable seats (Susan [19])---is that not characteristic of all churches; the building felt too spooky (Clare[22]); and she had no real opportunity to visit because she rarely strayed from the promenade (Alison B[27])! However, Evelyn [29] was able to recount a poignant tale of visiting the Cathedral with a blind person and after that person had touched the statues, carvings, and brass lectern, he was quite overcome by the whole aura of the nave. Peter[12], one of the more senior participants, had wartime recollections of the Cathedral and how its bell went silent for the duration of the hostilities, when a crack was discovered in the spire (of which I have been unable to find any more information, so I assume the sturdiness of the spire is without question), and when he thought he witnessed nuns in the cloisters. The latter is not consistent with my information concerning the nuns' residency, unless it is an actual confirmation of the myth that a ghostly nun still inhabits the place! While I am with Peter[ibid] and his wartime

75

reminiscences, I cannot forget his thrilling tale about Lachie McNeil, a local lad who was given a crucial role in keeping the area safe. He was stationed on the outer of the Eileans, armed with a red flag and, perhaps, a whistle. He was on U-boat watch and was to signal ashore if he spotted anything suspicious. One can sense the drama of the occasion, but little is known how many observations he actually achieved!

The suggestion that the Cathedral had previously not played a big role in the general community probably has some merit, but most people would acknowledge that there has been a definite shift in thinking and a positive outreach in recent years. Alison R[7] cites the example of the art studios that were developed in what was essentially an outbuilding and served to corral some of the growing artist colony on the Island. Wilson[8] noted with pleasure the fact that his son's wedding, which had earlier taken place in China, was blessed in the Cathedral when his own church in Millport was hesitant to provide it. The accommodation in the College has enabled a number of events to satisfy the community's thirst for music by featuring several residential weekends that have included public performances in the fields of opera and the classical guitar. In addition, the Sunday Classical Music concerts, so ably organized by Alastair Chisholm, are a joy to behold and attract sell-out crowds to those uncomfortable chairs! (Alison R[7]). In addition, the Cathedral has begun to offer delightful teas and dinners, some with topical themes, in the cloisters. They have been a great success due to the culinary arts and the ambience of the location. Children have been attracted to the trail of little faerie houses scattered through the dense woods fringing the buildings, and it appears that overnight those grounds, which might well have been aptly described as spooky once upon a time, have been opened up to all. (Fraser[32]).

It is fitting that we should leave the last word on the emerging exposure and importance of the Cathedral of the Isles to three of the Gallant Thirty Twa. Josh[17] brings an absolutely unique experience to the discussion, all the way from Texas, because the Cathedral will be forever associated with his place of birth in the local Lady Margaret Hospital. He has seen the records that confirm it and his baptism resides with others dating back to the early 1800s. That is heady stuff for a young American! He spent his first three years in and around the place and has visited it twice since returning to America. That has instilled in him an interest and joy in the history of the little cathedral. He marvels, as any true Texan would, in how small it actually is in comparison to all the giant churches back home; a little place but with a powerful message. Valerie[26], whom I met in her home in Canada, told me a great story about a dear expat friend, long settled in Canada, who remembered very little of her childhood in England except once she had attended a church camp in a cathedral in a place called Millport! I will leave Amanda[21] to provide a rich narrative of what the Cathedral has come to mean to her. Whereas she might once have felt it rather spooky, she now feels it to be "warm, peaceful, and serene." She attributes spending time in and around the Cathedral as the inspiration for her (blossoming in my opinion) photography career. Truly, a special place!

Here is another quirky little tale of Millport. There are currently 67 cities in the UK. The status is accorded by the Crown and no longer requires the existence of a cathedral although many of the cities have one. In 2011, some organization within Millport determined that it would be fitting for the town to become a city; after all it does have a cathedral. Alas, after further research, the application was abandoned. Had it been successful, Millport would have overtaken St David's in Wales as the smallest city in the UK. My own thoughts are that the word town aptly describes the place. City would have taken it somewhere else and suggested something far larger.

Chapter 9

The Shops

XI Greengrocer Hector McKinnon and his staff or is it his fan club!

There are many hamlets, villages, and small towns in Scotland with populations ranging between 500 and 3000 and they can reside on the mainland or on any one of the 94 populated islands around the country. By the way, there are more than 790 islands in total, so the vast majority are unpopulated. The Scottish Government classifies an area with a population of fewer than 3000 to be a remote rural area. Ergo, Great Cumbrae and Millport is a remote rural area. Furthermore, the Island, with its population of around 1300 ranks, number 10 of the 94 populated islands in contrast to Bute at 6500/5th and Arran at 4600/6th.

If one has occasion to visit a small town, which sounds much more inviting than a remote rural area to me, one is generally in for a treat. They usually have a character all of their own. Shaped by their history, they are mostly unspoiled, and they are alive, but only gently so! There will be a church, maybe two; there used to be a police station, but consolidation of the force has done away with that; there is in all probability a pub, there might even be two, in which case there will be something of a rivalry; and there will be a general shop, possibly doubling as a post office, carrying a little bit of most of life's essentials like foods, newspapers, lottery tickets, tobacco products (still), and most importantly, it will be licensed to sell alcohol. The general shop is the heartbeat of the town. It customarily offers news and gossip, free of charge, without any real need for the internet. Not that many years ago, there might have been three or four shops as well as businesses and workshops with an entrance for the public, like electrical and plumbing, but progress and different ways of doing business have whittled it all down to the computer and one shop. With that backdrop, we are going to examine the shopping experience in Millport, that remote rural area of 1300 people, oh and a deal more day visitors.

It is reported that in the 1920s, Millport had well over 100 shops! Even in 1960, there were over 50. Today, the number continues to dwindle and must be closer to 20. But the number is still phenomenally high compared to other similar towns and the history of shopping in the town is one that seems to resonate with people forever. The simple question posed to The Gallant Thirty Twa in the context of the shops was "which ones do you remember and why?". Boy did they respond, with endless lists being compiled. The challenge now for me was how to present the information. In the end, I have gone for analysis by street name (although Millport enjoys the distinction of having a continuous waterfront street that actually consists of five differently named streets with no obvious breaks or intersections!).

- *Frasers Gift Shop*
- *Alex Burnie Fishmonger*: Both Eric[3] and Donald & Jennie[11] were intrigued by the continuous controlled water running down the length of the window, presumably to keep the fresh fish fresh. You don't see thar feature these days but then again, you don't see many fish shops!
- *Whinfield Dairy*: This was the shop. The actual dairy was in Kames Bay. Christine[30] remembered being sent to pick up milk in the family jug, straight from the churn. On return home, it was placed in the "Osokool" chalk refrigerator. Clearly the Macraes were slightly ahead of their time!
- *Copeland/Cauldwell Newsagent*: Kyle[24] recalled this shop being the first port of call for ice cream after a strenuous afternoon of pier jumping into the harbour. Valerie[26], from further back, recalled the elderly Mr Copeland, with a cigarette hanging from his mouth, shooing the children out of the shop when they were trying to snag a free read of this week's comics.
- *Stewart & Kerr Fancy Goods*
- *J & M Kerr Souvenirs*
- *Hill's Dairy 1*

- *Hunters*: This shop, which we would know today as a delicatessen, was legendary and was recalled by every single participant. I remember the wooden counters, the absolutely packed shelves almost all the way to the ceiling, and the staff immaculately done out in old fashioned long starched white aprons. The shop appeared old fashioned and had been around, I think, since the 1920s, but its foodstuffs were anything but. Rather, they were exotic and came from many foreign lands, well at least I remember Holland and France! Everybody seemed to have a memory of the place---cheeses of varieties I had never heard of; Roses Lime Marmalade and Cremola Foam (Susan M[4]); the latter was a favourite of mine and the only time I ever got to drink it (was it not even available in that sophisticated capital of Edinburgh?); a high class establishment (Donald & Jennie[11]); a touch of class in the perfect Victorian setting (Bill[18]); "those beautiful mahogany counters and the giant meat cutter" (Alison R[7]); and "an extremely posh deli" (Alison B[27]). Clearly, everyone has been left with indelible memories of this shop, but I suspect that there is one more, overriding reason than those I have just mentioned. The owner, Steve Gourlay, was a dashing man with matinee idol looks (even I remember that!) and I think every woman on the Island made it their practice to visit the shop daily to make a purchase and have a chat with the man himself. And even better, if one bought enough to justify an order being made up, Steve would personally deliver it to the place of residence. All this went on. I kid you not. Quite a few of The Gallant Thirty Twa got misty-eyed at this part of the interview but I will not name them!

- *RJ Clark Jewellers*
- *Stark Pharmacy*
- *Templeton the Butcher*
- *Mills of Millport Clothing*
- *C & M Florence Fruit Shop*: A number of folks, including Wilson[8], spoke fondly of the proprietor, Charley Florence.
- *Fraser Electrical Services*
- *Kelly's Fruit Shop 1*

Guildford Street

- *JT McKay Grocer*
- *J & D McLachlan Fishmonger*
- *G & M Hastie Confections*
- *Mapes Cycles and Toys:* Mapes is another legend! Eric[3] remarked on the three generations of the family who ran the shop from its beginning and the fact that the couple who have recently taken it over have managed to maintain the outstanding reputation (as evidenced by the shop being named Bicycle Hire Shop of the Year 2022/23 by Scotland Prestige Awards). Alison R[7] has always been struck with the incredible window-shopping opportunity with toys and games for every age and taste. Eileen[13] was another to be amazed by the array of toys that always attracts children and adults who were once children! Mary[1] and Fraser[32] both mentioned the selection of fishing gear that was a must for children to acquire before

visiting the rock pools. I am pleased to note that today's children seem to be just as attracted to that particular activity.

- *E Morgan Bookie*: There were actually two bookies in town and apparently, they adopted a strange way of communicating results from the various racetracks in those days, before electronics made it a lot easier. They did good business as visitors sought ways to augment their holiday spending money. I remember being astonished when my mother disappeared into Mr Morgan's establishment one day. I later learned that she quite liked a flutter and in Edinburgh was able to place bets with the local newsagent! While on holiday that service was not available and so she had to go straight to source. Who would have thought it? Not me, certainly!
- *Anne Watt Draper*: This was a highly thought-of ladies' clothiers that attracted considerable business from the visitors. Bill[18] delightfully quoted the sign in the window---"This is the shop your friends have told you about"! Such gentile, subtle marketing! Fraser[32] recalled an aunt who held off making any purchases in the big city until she could get to Millport to Ms Watt's emporium to examine the latest models.
- *Walter Kerr Photographer*
- *The Sweet Shop*
- *The Co-op/VG Store/ Premier Store*
- *Hasties Confections*
- *McFarlane the Butcher*: Fraser[32] claimed this to be the location of the best sausages on the Island. It is interesting that there were three butchers competing for business in the town, and each had a name for a certain specialty. I am not sure if that meant that visitors called at all three during their morning sojourn to scoop up all the specialties or remained loyal to just one butcher. I suspect the loyalty factor was quite strong as it showed up in other places like bakers, grocers, chip shops, and pubs!
- *Colin Miller Hairdresser & Chemist*
- *Hill's Dairy 2*: Sandra[10] reminisced about getting milk in a jug, no need for bottles in those days before Brussels entered the picture! Clare[22] believed this shop to be the best place for a 10p mixture of sweets.

- *Miss Morton Millinery*
- *P&I Smith Toys*
- *JT Mackay Family Grocer*
- *Spiers the Baker 1:* This was another shop that carried legendary status at this location and their branch shop in Kames Bay. So many participants, myself included, remembered as children being sent to buy ultra-fresh rolls every morning. In fact, I think that the main reason I was readily provided with a hired bicycle for the duration of my holiday was so that I could be sent for rolls and newspapers! Others recalled the urge to pick up rolls either very late at night or very early in the morning when the shop was closed. No problem! One simply went around to the side of the building, knocked on the bakehouse door and was provided with what you wanted. It was obvious that it was the bakehouse because the outside wall was warm! There were so many tales about being sent to pick up the rolls that it is inevitable that this was the way that many of the participants had made their first acquaintance with one another, but it was only when they enlisted in The Gallant Thirty Twa that they became aware of it! Liz[14] said it for us all that it must have been a sad day on the Island when the Spiers family decided to up sticks and emigrate to South Africa. Though there were other good bakers, Spiers was never adequately replaced. Today the term "well-fired", as in half a dozen of the best, is probably not even understood!

Glasgow Street

- *Hector McKinnon Greengrocer:* Hector was another well-known purveyor in his shop and beyond. He enjoyed something of the same good looks as Steve Gourlay of Hunters, which meant he was popular with the ladies. He was also popular with everybody on the crowded Newton sands because he would wander from person to person offering toffee apples and slices of melon, as recalled by Alison B[27]. I can also affirm that both delicacies had a tendency to attract an accompanying layer of gritty sand and the occasional fly or wasp, but that did not impair their flavour!

- *Johnny Little Shoes*: This shop had two claims to fame. It was owned by the father of the Rangers footballer of the same name, and he was known to frequent the shop on occasion with some of his teammates. And the shop enjoyed the tradition of outfitting many a child with their summer sandals, a ritual that many looked forward to each year. I find it pleasing that this shop, one of three shoe shops in town, could engender enough trade to make it a viable business while contributing to the total holiday experience. "I know I am on holiday again because I just got my new sandals!" Alas, those days are no more.
- *Connells Licenced Grocery*
- *A & I Clark Confections*
- *Duncan Keith Sweets and Tobacco*: Duncan was a disabled gentleman who got about the shop with the aid of crutches. He showed great but not interminable patience with children who wanted to buy two-pence worth of sweets out of the jar on the top shelf. Just as he had struggled to replace the jar and moved to serve the next child, he would be met with "I would like the same please"!
- *Mary Miller Hairdresser*
- *MacKenzie Grocery*
- *Thomas Shields the Butcher*: Mary[1] tastefully recalled the regular order of Shields' famous steak pie for the family dinner. Clare[22] claimed this butcher was the maker of the best potted meat, a delicacy one does not hear so much about these days.
- *H Allan, Baker*
- *Ada Stewart Ladies & Children's Clothing*
- *St Clair Cameron, Baker*
- *Davie's Newsagent*: Peter[12] had memories of serving as the principal newspaper deliverer for this establishment during his war-time evacuation, whereupon he earned the princely sum of 3d per week! Davie's was also the location where accumulators for the low-tension current for "wirelesses" were charged. This was during WWII and long before the arrival of electricity to the Island, something that puzzled Peter[ibid]. He could only conclude that a generator was at work in the background somewhere.
- *James H Mackenzie, Grocer*

Kelburn Street

- *Dan Miller, Grocer*
- *Cumbrae Kitchen 2*
- *KB Grocer*
- *Wee Davie's Newsagent*
- *Spiers the Baker 2*

Other Locations

- *Cumbrae Kitchen 1 on Cardiff St.*
- *Burtt, Bookie on Reid Street*
- *Garden & Clark Coal Merchants on Clyde Street*
- *L & I Armour Grocery on Miller Street*
- *Bremner's Household Store on Cardiff Street*
- *Kate McIntyre on Crawford Street*
- *Kelly's Fruit Shop 2 on Cardiff Street*
- *Whinfield Dairy 1 on Ninian Street*

There you have it. Our group came up with a list of 60 shops and that was not them all; that was only the ones they could remember! It is quite amazing that so many shops were not only able to carve out a business but through their commitments to their customers were able to create living memories. In closing this chapter, it is worth quoting two observations that add to this picture of the shopping extravaganza available in this small town, later to become a remote rural area. Minia[31] and others happily recalled the window spotting competitions for children in the fifties and sixties and even to this day. Armed with a list of participating shops, children were charged with studying the contents of the shop windows in an exacting quest to find the item that did not belong with all the others; for example, a ring of black pudding tucked away surreptitiously among the toys and games. Locate all the odd-men-out and a prize could be yours! Minia[ibid] recalled that the late Sandy Morton had a good or bad reputation for making his odd-man-out extremely difficult to spot in his various shops that he operated.

This game is still practiced today but obviously the scope of the participating shops is much diminished. And that brings us back to the reality that today the changing DNA of the island visitor from a four week or more residence to more likely a day trip means that the need for so many shops has gone and will never return. However, in and among all the wistful reminiscences of the shops, I detected one of the few negative trends to emerge in discussing the Island of today. Quite a few of the participants were critical about some of the remaining shops and their failure to adequately serve the tourist population that remains. Too early closing in mid-afternoons, too many full days closed, too much inconsistency in operating hours were all cited as examples where visitors are being short-changed and first-time visitors are being given a bad impression that may cause them never to return. I think there is some validity in these comments. While it might be tempting for a shopkeeper on a quiet day to just pack it in and get an early night, especially after the visible day-trippers have started to disappear, there are still the visitors who are staying in rented accommodation or in their second homes to consider. It would be a great pity to see further diminishing of the shops on the front and Millport becoming just like those other small towns with very few amenities.

Chapter 10

Eats and Drinks

XII Ice cream or hot peas & vinegar at the Ritz Café.

Much like the plethora of shops in the previous chapter, Millport has enjoyed a high number of hotels and boarding houses, restaurants, and pubs relative to its size. And the number of each has altered as the pattern of visitors has changed from longer-term stays to day trips. Today one sees the exciting arrival of some new business ventures but a gradual overall reduction in facilities in line with the changing demographics.

The participants in this study were generally focusing their reminiscences on the heydays of the '50s, '60s, and 70s and it is sad to relate that many of those businesses no longer exist. However, they also made mention of current facilities and offered some favourable comparisons with the oldies.

As has been noted earlier, the small residential hotel and boarding house were popular accommodations when tourism was at its peak after WWII. In 1960, there were 14 such facilities in the town that tended to be favoured by frequently returning guests, who remained loyal to a particular establishment. The Millerston and The Towers in West Bay very much fell into that categorization. The Westborne, technically the only facility outside of the town but only just, has had short periods of great popularity, but its status has changed with respective ownerships, and it has fluctuated between a full-service hotel, boarding house, and bed and breakfast facility. Today all three establishments have gone back to what they probably originated as ----private residences. The Royal George Hotel, which recently shed its historic name for the Millport Pier Hotel, was probably always the premier hotel in town and now is the only hotel in town! Its imposing location at the head of the pier and harbour gives it obvious prominence and its services were frequently praised by participants in relation to accommodation, eating, drinking, and entertainment. In addition, the ownership seems to have acknowledged that prominence carries a community responsibility by playing an important part in local tourism and cultural affairs.

A very conspicuous hotel, that alas is no more, was the McGillivray Arms, which had another prime setting on Stuart Street across the square from the Royal George. Its ace card was its thriving bar which served as a focal point in the town. I enjoyed my first Millport drinks there at a tender age, which did not seem to unnerve the part-time barman. Harry Garden's other job at that time was the island policeman! Several of the participants fondly remembered the lively bar. Perhaps they even bore witness to David McNiven's impromptu performance on the piano that was referred to in a previous chapter. I remembered being shocked to arrive on the Island sometime in the '70s to find the hotel was gone and had been converted into luxury flats---a great loss to the community in some ways. The Mansewood was a somewhat similar establishment off the promenade on George Street. It had a reputation for being a bit wild at the weekend with discos and singing competitions. Mary[1] did not pull punches when she remembered it as "busy and noisy"! Ironically, its purpose has been changed into a special-needs care centre, which caters to a surprisingly large number of clients and is probably one of the Island's bigger employers. Minia[31] has already noted the convivial atmosphere in the Supper Room of the Clifton Boarding House on Marine Parade, where evening meals were rounded out with singsongs, something that was particularly popular in the '50s and '60s. The Cumbrae Club has also previously been noted. When the Kelly family took over ownership from Archie McCulloch and Kathie Kay, its popularity, if anything, even increased (Amanda[21]). A local combo provided dance music and the club was highly rated for its drinks and suppers. In particular, Susan B[19] recalled the popular chicken in a basket. Although I was never in the Cumbrae Club, I can fondly remember the same delicacy being offered in the Millerston Hotel up to 10 o'clock in the evening. That seemed almost Mediterranean in its timing and was the only place I can recall offering a late supper. Again, Millport to the forefront! Two other clubs have frequently offered drinks, meals, and entertainment up to the present day, those being the Golf Club and the Bowling Club. These events often take place, oddly enough, in the off-season for tourists and are really well supported by the permanent residents of the town. Suki[23] had good things to say about the theme nights such as Mexican Night at the former club, and particular entertainers being brought in at the latter club. In closing on the hotels, I feel that Millport could definitely do with at least a couple more hotels. Tourism numbers are on the increase and a new marina possibly to be constructed near the Old Pier, consequent to the already approved Flood Mitigation Plan, would bring a new kind of tourist, the boater. In other places where marinas already exist, they tend to support a healthy hotel business culture. The same should happen at Millport. Perhaps in due course, one or more of those former hotels will repurpose again. Who knows!

Other Clyde resorts, in fact resorts around the entire coast of the country, tend to have a strong drinking culture supported by numerous pubs. A feature of the holiday "doon the watter" from the big city was the high level of alcohol consumption and the occasional outbreaks of trouble. Millport does not seem to fit into that pattern. There are four dedicated pubs---Frasers, Twa Dugs formerly the Kelburne, Newton, and Tavern are all well run establishments with tremendously loyal patrons, both resident and visiting. Suki[23] was one who opined that the standards in the town far exceed other resorts she has visited and consequently there is far less trouble, particularly at closing time. Is there a favourite bar? I don't think so. The success of the bars is very much tied to their ownership and when change occurs there appears to be a tendency to hark back to the old days. The Twa Dugs and Tavern seem to be going through that phase right now. In their own way, each bar is very active in attracting customers while at the same time encouraging specific purpose gatherings. Suki[ibid] made an amusing observation about the Tavern where on a given night the bar was hosting a lively music evening, a Christian group meeting, and a bingo session. She remarked that the interaction in the communal toilets was quite interesting! Frasers and the Newton are noted for the quality of their menus but then they differ with the former being a really friendly place for gathering and conversation while the latter presents some of the best music acts in the town in its spacious lounge bar. I remember Josh[17] mentioning something that is dear to my heart, the amazing collection of photographs of just about every steamer that ever sailed the Clyde which adorns the walls of Frasers. If the conversation begins to drag a little, one can always wander about reading the captions on the photographs and getting an instant history lesson for free! All in all, I think the Island is well served for public houses and they are doing a good job to meet the public's needs. One thing that surprised me in the interviews was almost one third of the participants did not have an awful lot to say about the pubs at all because they do not drink. And this in Scotland!

The Gallant Thirty Twa put their heads together and came up with 18 past and present eating places in Millport. That is not a bad number and appears to allow for a good deal of choice. Yes and no! We will go into that later on. Arguably the most popular restaurant was the Ritz Café, once the proud recipient of an award for the best ice cream in Scotland and strongly endorsed by Clare[22]! It also had a somewhat unusual but highly prized reputation for deluxe hot peas and vinegar (Donald & Jennie 11 and Alison B[22])! I have partaken of the delicacy, but my sceptical Canadian wife has yet to be persuaded. In all honesty, I have never seen the dish offered elsewhere. It is either unique to the Island or a not very common dish emanating from Glasgow; that would be my guess. The Ritz was always packed, regardless of the weather, because it was an attraction for day trippers in particular. And on those odd wet days, it was packed, and never seemed to empty, at least until the rain ceased. Seona & Gordon[5] remarked on their amazing forbearance to make a single coke last the duration of a rain shower! Some of that time could also be spent, as Clare[22] recalled, looking for the single triangle hidden within the crazed pattern of the Formica table tops. Going back to the ice cream, it certainly enjoyed a great reputation. Clare[ibid] believed it to be the best available and Josh[17] has a lasting memory of the ice cream with the raspberry sauce drizzled over the top, apparently a delicacy not freely available in Texas! The previously mentioned Andy's Snack Bar, aka Beachcomber, in the Garrison also enjoyed a reputation similar to the Ritz and later it morphed into the Nixe on the square at the pier. The Nixe boomed as the haven for young people in contrast to the more family-oriented Ritz. For a few years in the '60s, never a day went by without me visiting the Nixe for an ice-cold coke and a hamburger with onions if I was feeling flush. I never once witnessed an incidence of trouble; the owners Martha and Andy were way too cool to countenance such a thing, so I was surprised when Alison R[7] expressed her preference for the Ritz because the Nixe "was considered too rough" How could it ever be termed rough? In that Summer of Love, 1967, we were all too engrossed in listening to "San Francisco" on the Nixe jukebox and espousing peace and love to ever cause any trouble!

Along the other end of town, the Kames Bay Café and the Swiss Café drew rave reviews. They were particularly popular with tourists who were lodging in the East Bay. Everywhere one looked in Millport, one saw strong loyalties, largely based on geographical considerations. In addition, Minia[31] was grateful that the Kames took orders and then delivered them to people on the beach---a very nice service unlikely to be encountered anywhere today. Christine[30] attempted to share with me an explanation of the Kames Bay attitude and how it translated into loyalty to all the different facilities in that neighbourhood. I was left mentally comparing it to the Valley Girl phenomenon of the 1980s that started in the USA but kind of spread world-wide. I wonder if she agrees with that analogy! I am not sure I was ever in the Swiss and I was only ever in the Kames when it was combined with a putting game or a visit to that beach. As in the case of the cafes at the other end of town, the popularity of the Swiss and Kames was directly attributable to the families who owned and operated them. The Fairhaven Café on the east side and Fintry Bay Café on the west were highly loved stopping-off points on a ride or walk around the Island. While the former is no longer with us, the latter has transformed into a modern facility on the other side of the road from the original tin hut, and has very recently progressed from a café into a full-blown restaurant. This is the kind of progression that bodes well for the Island.

There have always been several tea shops in Millport. In fact, I think this has been quite common in many coastal resorts. Their offerings were often more limited than a café and they sought to portray a more gentil image where decent people could sit quietly sipping coffee or tea and discussing the ways of the world or maybe the latest gossip permeating the town! The Tea Room in the Square, Ye Olde Tea Shoppe, and the Garrison Tea Room were all remembered by the participants, and yet I got the sense that nobody was particularly a regular attender. Perhaps that is the reason why none of these establishments has remained to this day. But at least Starbucks has not yet made a foray into this island's life!

Was it in the 1970s that ethnic restaurants exploded upon Scotland and eventually led to chicken tikka marsala overtaking the ubiquitous fish and chips as the most popular dish in the country? Millport was no exception! It has enjoyed The Golden Dragon (Chinese) and Spice Island (Indian) and both attracted tremendous custom among tourists and residents, as recalled by many of the participants. The former is still going strong after a change of ownership and the latter, which ultimately closed, is now being touted for a return, much to the delight of Clare[22] and others. I guess one can throw the current pizza restaurant in as another ethnic option. These popular options illustrate the changing tastes of the Millport consumer and also the changing DNA of today's tourists. Having mentioned them, we cannot ignore the importance of the fish and chip shop, whose presence is virtually mandatory in every single coastal resort. Millport had three to choose from in the heydays. The Deep Sea has a prime location next door to the Royal George Hotel at the pierhead and thrives to this day, judging by the length of the queues out of the door at certain times. Fraser[32] noted that it remains the first port-of-call when his family hits the island---pick up suppers on their way to their mobile home. I have made something of a joke about appointing myself as the ultimate fish and chip researcher searching literally around the world for the perfect supper. Thus far, and without fear of bias, I can state that, in spite of changes in ownership over the years, the fish supper in the Deep Sea remains the best. That should stir things up no end! The Crocodile Chippy across from the iconic rock, presently between owners, also enjoys a good reputation and I think benefits from that old loyalty thing. It is a long way for Kames Bay residents to walk to the pier, so the nearby shop does very well. The third shop is no more and there is probably no way that it ever could be in this era of heightened health and safety. Not far from the Crocodile, there existed a chip shop up a close (you all know what that is, a stairway that generally leads to private flats, not commercial activities) and that shop operated an open fat-fryer on a domestic cooker/stove for the preparation of its offerings! Can you picture it? The heat it must have given out! The dangers it presented! Bill[18] predicted the unusual form of frying had never changed since the 1920s and yet he, as well a number of other participants, swore by it and claimed the product was the absolute best. This world-wide researcher never sampled a supper there so I cannot comment but there is no doubt it enjoyed an awesome reputation. The shop might have been associated with the nearby Swiss Café or not, but alas both have disappeared. But folks will never forget that open fat-fryer!

We turn now to some other relatively new restaurants that were not around in what I term the heydays but are familiar to the participants. The Dancing Midge burst upon the scene on Glasgow Street by way of a reality show on television that was tracking people who had decided to opt out of the rat race and pursue something completely different in their lives. An unlikely candidate was a couple with a hankering to set up a small restaurant in Millport! The restaurant was and has continued to be a success, although the original owners decided to drop out after a few years. Fortunately, the spirit with which the Midge was created seems to have been sustained, although at least one of the participants felt it has lost something, particularly in terms of consistency of opening hours---but more of that Millport malaise in a little while. The Round Island Café is another newcomer which has carved out a good reputation for serving tourists and putting on a reasonable show in the off-season when only permanent residents tend to be looking for a meal. That leads us to our final restaurant; Minstrels was a successor to the Nixe, in that prime site at the pierhead, and quickly became arguably the most popular eating place on the Island. Its menu and ambiance were definitely a step up from a seaside café and it enjoyed the patronage of tourists and residents alike. I have to admit it was my favourite, and I shamelessly plugged it by name in several of my novels. Unfortunately, it first became a short-term casualty of the pandemic, then a long-term casualty, and now it still remains closed when virtually every other establishment is fully operational again. At the time of writing, its future is completely uncertain. That has brought adverse reaction in the research for this book. Minstrels was a great favourite among many of the participants, who now are expressing frustration with its limbo status. And it is a similar frustration to that expressed in relation to the erratic operating hours and early closing that other restaurants and shops continue to exhibit. This appears to be a classic dilemma. The owners may feel it is not worth staying open as they did in the past because they cannot make sufficient revenue but if their operating hours continue to be shortened or just simply erratic, their revenues may continue to fall---a case of the self-fulfilling prophecy. These are challenging times for this business sector on the Island, possibly more so than for any other. There are heart-warming new success stories but yet, increasingly negative indicators.

Chapter 11

Sporting and Other Events

XIII Crazy Golf in the prime setting on the promenade.

Whatever families tended to do when they were at home, and it probably varied according to where they lived, once they were in Millport it was outdoor activities all day long. Staying inside whatever accommodation they had was only contemplated on wet days and even then, only as a last resort. If it is amazing that there are so many activities going on today, then it is almost mind-boggling how many activities were happening back in the heydays and were so fondly remembered by members of the Gallant Thirty Twa! Events of every conceivable type were put together by an amazing organization that existed for that very purpose; or were arranged by specific event groups; or were organized by visitors; or just seemed to happen almost of their own accord. And happen they did on a daily basis during the main Fair fortnights and thereafter on every weekend of the season. We will visit just some in order to whet the reader's appetite, but the best thing to do is to get over to the Island oneself and experience the events that still remain.

The Development Association was an extraordinary organization funded, I expect, by the local council that hired a few students from Glasgow to spend the summer break from their studies on the Island. They had a very specific mandate---to conceive and organize an amazing array of activities for the visitors and to do it in a funny and friendly way. They smacked a little of the red coats or blue coats at the holiday camps (remember them?) but without the cheesy uniforms. Their hut on the promenade, covered in handbills advertising upcoming events, was immediately remembered by most participants, particularly Donald & Jennie[11] and Liz[14]. Seona & Gordon[5] recall it being the very place you consulted if you had a specific interest in an event but in truth a great many people just wandered by the hut to see what was on today and that week. And if you could not get close to the hut, which was often the case, many of the events were also featured on handbills displayed in shop windows, in pubs, and on every available space of wall in the town. If it transpired that you had missed an event you had been interested in, well it really meant you must have been walking around with your eyes closed! Many of the events were put on in the DA Hall in the Garrison grounds and I always assumed DA was some sort of military acronym, a bit like TA for the Territorial Army. It should have been obvious. It was named after the illustrious Development Association! The Association organized every conceivable activity including the beauty contests on the beach for teens and children (where Alison B[27] took first place in the latter, I have been told to mention!); the search for the glamorous grannies (a seriously contested affair where reputations were made and lost); sandcastle competitions where children with no little help from dads created elaborate edifices; the stiff tennis competitions mentioned earlier and relished by Bill[18]; the races round the Island, be it walking, running, or on bikes where Bill[ibid] still claims a healthy record of 38 minutes on two wheels, and I guess he can without fear of dispute, for no records were kept that I have seen; the go as you please competitions (talent competitions I think before Simon Cowell learned how to make money out of them) fondly remembered by Sandra[10] and Valerie[26]; a Millport variant on the It's a Knockout television show put on in West Bay Park and recalled by Alison B[ibid]; and the fancy dress competitions. I assure you that these are only a sample but what more could you ask for? Well, there is more to come. As previously noted, football has always been a big thing on the Island. The pitch in West Bay featured games every few days, including the Millport Amateurs contesting the Finlayson Cup, a solely island-based competition, against similar sides from resorts around the Clyde. On special occasions they would play professional sides like Rangers, St Mirren, and Queens Park when they were on a summer break between seasons and even the City of Glasgow Police side. No chance of trouble breaking out at that game, or was there? If you look closely at the photograph on page 84 of Hector McKinnon and his harem, you will see in his window the handbill for the upcoming visit of Queens Park! And when the men's team had nothing else to do, they would play their weekly games against The Visitors, consisting of whomever had come a-visiting and had chosen to try out for the representative side. I remember these being very closely contested games, perhaps because there was always the rumour of there being a ringer or two in the visiting side. You will recall that several Rangers players liked to visit the Island! Can you imagine that happening now? The entire Development Association budget for the whole summer would not be able to cover the insurance premium for one highly-valued foreign player, even if he were keen to show his stuff! But that is not the complete story of the football in West Bay. Long before it seemed to get organized anywhere else, Millport had its ladies' team as well, made up of keen and cute locals who all wore their jerseys outside of their shorts just like 'Slim' Jim Baxter! They too played on a weekly basis against that illustrious side, "The Visitors". These games were more than just a game on the field. They were an event. The teams were paraded to the field on a horse and cart belonging to Harry Garden the local coal merchant (and also of police officer and part-time barman fame). You could tell the source because Harry never did a great job of cleaning up the cart and more than one player would leap off it to reveal a decidedly black bottom! Maybe that was why they insisted on wearing their jerseys outside their shorts. The man himself, Harry if you are following, served as referee for most games and like the referees of today was known to give the odd controversial decision if one team needed a bit of help. He was not, however, a homer by any means; he could upset either team or even both teams during a game. Consequently, there was a time-honoured tradition that immediately after the game, irrespective of the result, the man in black (there is a pun there, remember his profession as well as his vocation!) would be unceremoniously dumped in the nearby boating pond. He took it all in his stride; perhaps it was quicker than showering after a day's labour; and he was always ready for the next game and the next ritual. It was great fun and attracted big crowds stretched out around the field on all four sides. I could watch it all from the window of Kimberley House where my family stayed. It was a bit like a forerunner to the corporate boxes in the stadiums of today. However, I much preferred being out and about in the middle of the fun. I never got to play for The Visitors but much later in life I was quite shocked to hear my brother Ian make a claim that he had been "capped". That revelation I could not remember and again because no records are available, I will have to concede that one to him. The football was so popular and there were so many memories that it could justify a book in its own right. Liz[14], like Ian, was proud to recall that she had played for The Visitors and in her case, I have no reason to doubt her. Sandra[10] recalled the competitiveness of the Finlayson Cup games and if a mid-week tie was drawn and had to go to extra time, well the visiting side missed the last steamer! No problem. In would step the omnipresent Stewart McIntyre to ferry them back in his boat and thereby make yet another notable contribution to the Island community spirit. And finally, Harry-in-the-pond is a lasting memory for so many who witnessed those days; he was another character!

The two most well-established sports with their own facilities are bowling and golf. The two clubs have each been around for well over 100 years and have enjoyed continued success with their peaks probably coinciding with the Island heydays after WWII. Both clubs have a thriving social side which extends beyond the players and can involve good food and beverages and entertainment. I particularly remember winning the tombola at the annual Bowling Club fete! In the period which the participants focused on, it seems like quite a high percentage of men came to Millport year after year in order to play bowling or golf on just about every day of their holiday. In all likelihood, their practice while at home was to pursue their favourite game at the weekend only while they were working on weekdays. To be able to dedicate 14 or 28 days strictly to their game must have felt like a dream come true. The bowling season was punctuated with special matches involving visiting teams from the west of Scotland and none was bigger than the modestly entitled "Millport versus The Rest of the World" match! John[6] recalled the splendour of the teams arriving off the steamer nattily attired in matching blazers, flannels, white shirts and club ties. Only the blazers were removed when play began! I can remember in very recent years encountering the Millport team returning from a game on the mainland, and they were similarly dressed. Obviously, the tradition continues. John[ibid] also remembers other days when a wappenshaw was held at the club. I am reliably informed that a wappenshaw is unique to Scotland and is a drop-in tournament where an open draw is made among the arrivals without any seeding. It then continues on a knockout basis until a winner emerges. Bowling generally has been seen as struggling in recent times to attract as many young players as possible to replace the older players dropping out of the sport. However, in the heydays it was hugely popular. Donald of Donald & Jennie[11] remembered his dad commenting that he played in Millport with a large number of players from Paisley, but though he lived in that city, he did not know any of them in the bowling circles of Paisley. He would not see them again until holiday-time in the following year! Golf has always been popular on the Island, to this day. Fraser[32] recalled the daily meeting in the Garrison grounds of several families before the men set off for their regular tee-time up the hill. This went on for six days per week. On Sunday, no play was then permitted, which gave Fraser and his pals the opportunity to walk the course and search for lost golf balls, He estimated that they generally found around 400 over a month but he did not say whether there was a market in selling them or they were merely used to replace their own lost balls over the holidays! The boards in the clubhouse that list the champions of the various tournaments make interesting reading. Again, during the heydays, I was able to recognize the names of most of the star scratch amateur golfers from all over Scotland, who went on to play in the Walker Cup and often turned professional with great success, all after their little sojourns to Millport. I enjoyed the stories about bowling and golfing and have to report what I thought was the funniest. John[6], the avid, indeed champion bowler, visited me in Millport to do his interview and was setting foot on the Island for the first time in over 40 years! The memories flooded back to him on all things to do with bowling. However, when I asked him if he had ever played golf as well, he gave me a deadpan answer "I didn't know there was a golf course on the Island". The more I think about it, I wonder if he was winding me up!

There is also a long list of events that are organized by groups of enthusiasts. Millport and the Isle of Cumbrae seems to be just the perfect location. For example, the classic cars from all over the country descend on the Island for one weekend. They set up in the Garrison grounds, all polished up with their hoods open for the aficionados to examine them and drool a little as well. Then, at a specific time, a long line of cars of all vintages will set off on a parade around the coastal road. It is quite something to see. Similarly, the scooter rally lasts a full weekend. Hundreds of mods, and I mean real mods from the 1960s, many of whom will not see their personal 60s again, descend on the Island suitably attired in parkas, checked pants, and moccasins. Those who still have hair even have those cool haircuts with the front short and the top back-combed just as the Small Faces would have wanted it. But I dwell too long on the humans, it is the scooters that are to be admired as well--- Vespas, Lambrettas, many more lovingly restored originals than the new copies from China. And the more mirrors one can hang on them the better. Their weekend is spent strutting about, in the true sense of the word, parking in giant clusters outside pubs, standing talking scooter business (there is even the ability to have repairs or modifications done on the spot) and then every so often they take off on a round-the-island parade just like the cars. One time I saw it and there were even some Harley Davidson motorcycles that had snuck into the parade. Thankfully there was no repeat of the confrontations of Southern England in the 1960s. Mods and rockers have learned finally to co-exist! In the evenings, in the big marquee in the Garrison grounds, wild dances featuring the music of the times round out an amazing weekend. And they keep coming back year after year!

The most notable event, mentioned earlier in the chapter on music, is the Country & Western Music Festival. It is much more than just an outdoor festival. It takes over the entire island. And the locals get involved too, unlike some of the other events. Businesses dress up and adopt new western identities. There are more Stetsons and American flags than one would see anywhere outside Texas, according to Josh[17]. Events, both official and unofficial, take place throughout the town. The majority of outdoor performances are now centred in the Garrison, but Seona & Gordon[5] could remember when events also took place in West Bay and Kames Bay. It certainly has put the Island on the map over the years; I realized that when I heard 'Whispering' Bob Harris extol its virtues on BBC Radio 2 no less! Finally, the town grasps the opportunity to dress up again for the September Weekend, the traditional closure to the holiday season, with flickering padella lights illuminating the specially decorated windows in businesses and private homes as noted by Mary[1] and Eric[3]. If you get the impression that this is a town that enjoys dressing up, I can also add that in recent years there has been a Victorian Weekend where great-grandma's long-since abandoned clothing has made a celebrated return according to Wilson[8].

Inevitably many of the activities on an island focus on the water that surrounds it. There are crazy raft races, involving mainly residents who are tasked with building from whatever materials come to hand, crafts of ingenious design that will win the all-out race from Kames Bay to the harbour. Competition is fierce. Seona & Gordon[5] recall water bombs being adopted by the more unscrupulous crews. In the end, there are far fewer finishers than began the race, with frequent capsizings being the scant reward for a year's labour building the rafts. Still, there is always next year to look forward to! There is also the New Year Loonie Dook when the bravehearted, and in some cases seriously hungover, risk life and limb to take the plunge in Kames Bay. Again, this is mainly an event for residents but Alison R[7] and Wilson[8] were keen to reminisce about it without revealing if they had actually taken the plunge. In reality, on even the hottest summer day, Kames Bay water is fiercely cold so I am not sure that it gets any worse on the first day of the year! A variation on the Dook which can only happen at certain times and not every year is the walk to the Eileans. Walk you say? An exceptionally low tide permits the occasional walk from Newton Beach to the islands in Millport Bay. Usually, some exposure to the water is required but if the tide is low enough, the journey can be completed without resorting to swimming. The view back toward the town is stunning and, in the absence now of the little boats for hire, it is probably the only way the view can be accomplished. I have never done the walk, but I do recall at high tide on a really wet day in the '60s, my friends and I swam out to the Eileans to test the scientific theory that the water is warmer when it is raining. The target was achieved but the theory proved inconclusive. Even after reviving Bovrils in Andy's Snack Bar, we could not make up our minds! A much more ambitious, indeed impressive, swim takes place every year from the slip at the Water Sports Centre directly across to the beach at Largs. While it is the shortest point between the Island and the Mainland, it is still the daunting equivalent of 110 lengths of a 25m swimming pool. Alison R[7] informed me with some pride that she was one of the nine hardy souls who took part in the first ever swim. Today the event attracts about 100 participants. When I witnessed the most recent one, I marvelled at the jocularity and tenacity of all the swimmers. After all, it is not like a road race, one cannot just drop out at the half-way stage if not at your best that day! And there are still more water activities to report. Parents and children have forever fished their hearts out around the coast of Cumbrae, some with expensive equipment and others with a simple net. I am not sure how much catching goes on but there were always favourite spots that were reckoned to be more productive than anywhere else. Fraser[32] posits that just off Farland Point was always the best spot and judging by the number of anglers who still go there, he just might be right. At one time there was also the hugely popular fishing parties that would go out each evening, but more of that in a minute. If one prefers to just look at fish rather then hook them, the Robertson Aquarium that is attached to what is now the Field Studies Centre, is a good place to study the mysteries of the deep (and the Clyde has a wonderful selection). The Aquarium has been around for over 100 years and still draws the curious or the bored on a wet day (Eric[3]).

One of the great attractions in Millport right up to about the 1980s was the boat hirers based on one of two jetties on Newton Sands. While the number of companies went up and down over the century, there being as many as four for much of the time, there seemed always to be the Old Firm of boat hirers----Hunters and Mauchlines. It was a grand rivalry that was carried on by residents and visitors alike. Loyalty was paramount; for example, if all the Hunter boats were booked, the very last thing one would do as a Hunter-man would be to take out a Mauchline boat even if it were available. Both firms offered rowing boats and little motorboats. No prior experience was necessary, one just paid the modest fee, jumped in, and a life on the ocean wave beckoned! I never saw a lifejacket in evidence. Perhaps that is one of the reasons why no such services exist now on the beach, with the exception of the kayaks for hire at On Your Bike (and they come with life jackets!) All the hire companies engaged what seemed like a huge amount of volunteer youths to operate their businesses. I don't think any money changed hands, but it was seen as a great honour to be part of a team. Many kids spent the majority of their holidays "working on the boats". Now, just try getting them to do some work at home! Spencer[16] shared with me a nipper of a story about his brother who helped out with one of the hire companies. When a woman left her handbag in her rowing boat after it had been returned, he was polite enough to pick it up and run after her to return it. But not before popping a little crab in to be discovered later on! Hunter and Mauchline also ran big open launches that went on excursions to nearby resorts in the afternoon and took out the fishing parties in the evenings. These trips were generally sold-out if a booking was not made the day before! I was never a great fan of the latter as I never ever caught a fish even though they were being hauled aboard to the right of me and to the left of me. My brother Ian graciously offered to give me one of his and say I had caught it, but I declined. That was not really the point, was it! The fishing parties were a great draw for the many people who lived in the big cities and had no exposure to fishing. It was the highlight of many a holiday and might have been the very reason for my family choosing Millport as its favoured location because my mother's sister and her husband made the trip from Edinburgh each year solely for the fishing!

Almost every weekend in the season, a wild group of some sort, dressed in loud commemorative tee-shirts, lands on the Island to do a walk or run or ride for a charity. The place is perfect for this activity and groups come from far and wide. One can generally hear them before they are seen because there is so much hooting and hollering. It is just the way fund-raising should be---fun---and afterwards most groups end up in one of the pubs to also help the island economy. As unusual as these events can be, surely one of the most unusual, as recalled by Minia[31], was the effort to push a hospital bed right around the Island in aid of raising funds for a health charity. Now that kind of four-wheel vehicle seems quite acceptable to me; it is just the cars I have this thing about! Talking about four of a set, I should mention another very popular pastime that is making a bit of a comeback today. Horses and ponies (they have four legs, yes!) were extremely popular on Newton Sands and Kames Bay beach, while there was also trekking on the then quiet roads of the Island. Children, particularly little girls for some reason, were always keen on riding. And many also volunteered at the stables to feed and water the animals and walk them down to the beach. Mary[1], Spencer[16], Clare[22], and Evelyn[29] were all effusive in their memories of how the children flocked to the riding and Liz[14] was pleased to note her daughters and others had a great experience in the stables even if it was hard work.

There just remain some memories of impromptu events that simply sprung up, generally starting with a parent trying to amuse his own kids and ending up with that parent overseeing a full-on competition with lots of other kids while their parents could lope off to the nearest pub! Five-a-side football frequently sprung up this way, and once fully organized, a little family kick-around progressed into the World Cup. Moira[28] and Evelyn[29] recalled their father starting a little game of rounders to amuse them in West Bay Park. Children from all angles flocked to join the game and at its conclusion everybody wanted to know when the next game would take place. Funnily enough, this past summer I witnessed what must have been half a dozen families of children and parents playing a massive game of rounders in West Bay and having a whale of a time. The tradition continues but Millport may be the only place in the world where rounders is still played! Moira[ibid] and Evelyn[ibid] had a similar tale to tell from the boating pond where that gregarious father of theirs introduced a little competition where the

104

sisters could race their toy yachts. You can guess what happened next, and so the daily childrens' yachting regatta, open to all, was begun!

And so ends this chapter of events and activities. There have been so many I am almost fatigued just thinking about them. Without a doubt, families made the very most of their holidays in Millport. Oh sure, there was a lot of lolling around the beaches too. Why else would there be so many deckchairs for hire? But people liked to be active most of the time and they had amazing choices of what to do. I will leave it to Tracy[15] to come up with a little slogan that describes it well:

"Embrace the Millport way of life, which means participating in as many events as possible".

Hear Hear!

Chapter 12

Why Do We Keep Returning?

XIV Pony rides on the Newton Sands.

There were no real qualifications for becoming one of The Gallant Thirty Twa other than having been associated with the Island at one time or another and generally remaining as an occasional visitor as opposed to being a permanent resident. However, what transpired from the discussions with the participants was that in most cases there was a long history of coming to Millport through multiple generations of families and the prospect that the practice would continue into the future in spite of changing interests and values. The purpose of this chapter was to attempt to determine if there were common reasons why this should be so. A social scientist would have had a field day as memories and opinions rolled out!

Well over half of the participants revealed that two or more generations in the family have been Millport visitors on a fairly consistent basis. Five of the families extended to four generations and three reported five generations. Think about five generations of a family. How about grandchild, child, parent, grandparent, and great-grandparent. That is quite a spread, probably close to 100 years. In many cases, not only were there multiple generations caught up in this love affair with the Island, but their visits were undertaken at the same time. Consequently, some of these room and kitchen flats could get pretty congested during the holidays. But nobody seemed to mind. There was a sense of togetherness that was very strong. A good many respondents stated, for example, that the holiday would just not be complete without Granny being present as the all-imposing matriarch who still had time to spoil the children. There were several references to generations handing down to the next generation the values and traditions that went with a simpler life spent in Millport for at least two weeks each year, and how the thoughts of the following year to come kept them going in their very different lives back home. With societal changes appearing to be much more rapid these days, one can only wonder if that handed-down philosophy is sustainable. One can only hope so for the future mental well-being of the visitors and for the sake of the Island as we know it and love it.

In addition to inter-generational families, quite a common occurrence seems to have been separate and otherwise unrelated families coming together to spend annual holidays in Millport. They could stay together by taking over a big house or arrange near-to-each-other digs that allowed for similar communal living. This involved the several female adults doing the coffee and shopping circuit in the morning, no doubt with a visit to Hunters Grocers, while the several male adults took to the bowling greens or golf course. And a collective of children could be quite formidable. Hunting as a pack was a phrase used by a couple of the participants to describe the gatherings as they sought adventures of all types from morning, afternoon, and into the long summer evening after they had returned home briefly only to be fed and watered! Wilson[8] noted just how resourceful the children in Millport are in creating their own entertainment and the traditions seem to have continued in spite of the arrival of instant electronic entertainment. And the amazing thing was that these families often came from widely dispersed cities and never got together at any time other than the summer holidays. The only contact in the off-season was to make sure that everyone was available and up for next year's plans. They usually were! A slight variation on this multi-family arrangement was the practice of families going back to the same accommodation each year and discovering the same people they had met last year and in previous years. In this case, there was no conscious intent to make prior arrangements; it just happened organically through each family having basically the same values and traditions. It is quite intriguing how powerful these practices appear to have been. I must admit I had no real experience of them other than one or two members outside the immediate family joining our family in the early years. After that it was down to just my family and eventually to just me and my own newly acquired family. That still makes for three generations, so we still manage to fit within the statistics!

There was one predominant reason why so many of the participants described themselves as frequent visitors to the Island. It all had to do with the feeling of serenity that just arriving there induced, and also the overriding feeling of safety, particularly in respect to children. That is it in a nutshell. More than one participant expressed the sense of Cumbrae representing old world mentality, meaning to step on the Island was to escape from the real world and back into something much simpler where only good things happen (Moira[28]). Josh[17] and Mark K[20] noted that they felt any stress they carried to the Island disappeared immediately when they set foot on it. This is especially poignant for Josh, a young man whose regular home is in the hustle and bustle of Houston, Texas. For him to detect the psychological change means that in spite of his background, he immediately becomes at one with the other visitors when he is here. That impact was also noted by Donald & Jennie[11], Tracy[15], and Bill[18]. Amanda[21] could remember her father noticeably shedding all signs of tension the minute he stepped on the ferry from Largs. Although he travelled all over, he expressed the view that he never found the same sense of community and serenity anywhere else. That, of course, is similar to my good self. As I mentioned at the beginning of this book, for the longest time I thought I was the only one blessed with this feeling of euphoria on that eight-minute ferry ride to my spiritual home. But I am not possessive. I am now more than willing to share the feeling now that I am aware of its broader influence!

Another important reason for the annual pilgrimage was offered by Sandra[10], and that is she believes holidays on the Island are wholesome healthy holidays. That is a reason that seems to be much more important today than it was back in say the '60s, but that is only because there is much greater consciousness and dialogue in these times. I don't suppose people deliberately went to Millport because it was a healthy place to be. They were just happy to benefit from a fortuitous consequence of their visits and it felt good to repeat them.

The sense that the Island has almost Zen qualities for all those stressed-out adults is further enhanced by the belief, held by so many I talked to, that it is the ultimate safe haven for children. Back in the heydays, it was virtually de rigueur for children to disappear from the home after breakfast, find young relatives or friends, old or just made yesterday, and to embark on adventures for the entire day. Tracy[15] cited the fun activities as the very epitome of the Island visit. The day was only interrupted by the need to return home for meals. The majority of children did not wear a watch because it could meet a disastrous end when the left hand was plunged into the rock pools looking for crabs or other treasures. How did they know that it was time to return for meals? There must have been something in the stomach juices that just signalled the time was right for sustenance. I know I never missed a meal irrespective of where I had strayed off to! One can understand children's desires to make the most of all that was on offer and what seemed to be so different from the things to do at home. But it is really interesting how most parents went along with the practice and assumed that their children were safe and in no fear of harm. John[6] and Liz[14] were but two who admitted they had no real concerns throughout the day and Mark K[2] echoed the sentiment but freely noted that parents where he came from in London would never have dreamt of letting the kids do the same thing in the big city. So many participants described

Millport as a "safe haven" for children. Now one might argue that was then and this is now. Society seems to have changed in regard to child welfare, and not for the better. There are so many sordid tales of abuse toward children in the media every day. Surely this "laissez-faire" attitude has disappeared even from Millport? I look around all the places of adventure today, the rock pools, the beaches, the harbour, the parks, not to mention the road chock-a-block with bicycles---and I see very few parents in evidence. It seems that the philosophy that the kids are safe and free to do whatever they fancy is alive and well on this self-contained island environment. And the funny thing is that many of the parents, when one does actually encounter them, have changed from the old days. New races and cultures have discovered this secret place. Languages other than Glaswegian and English are commonplace! But the philosophy endures. It really is quite encouraging that there just might be hope for society! The continuance of Paradise was well and succinctly described by Seona & Gordon[5], Wilson[8], and Eileen[13]---"Kids love Millport, then they grow out of it at some stage and discover other places, and then they rediscover it just in time to introduce it to their own kids!" Amanda[21] personalized this tendency by saying when she entered her twenties, she abandoned the Island for a while to explore other places. Now she is back and becoming a permanent resident.

One word that kept coming up among the participants when I pressed them for the single magical reason why they kept returning to the Island was "familiarity". That could have been a somewhat negative response along the lines of "same old same old". It clearly wasn't! As a couple said "It never changes but you never want it to. It gets into your blood!" There cannot be a lot of places where visitors feel like they are home. One can understand that feeling developing in residents after a while but for temporary residents, some only on the Island for two weeks per year, it is surely a rare feeling. Tracy[15] talked about lasting friendships being formed as a result of repeated weekend visits. Bill[18] mentioned several friendships within the entertainment business that he became part of, yet those friendships were first forged in Millport at as early as 13 years of age. Fraser[32] shared a charming story of his daughter doing a primary school project on what she had done for her holidays. The extensive report on the joys of Millport was well received by her teacher, who just happened to be a habitual visitor as well! An

A grade was inevitable! And Mark K[20] perhaps best described what it means to be accepted as an Island visitor. Although he has a place in the Crosshouse at the beginning of the East Bay and the nearest newsagent is located no more than 100 yards from it, he states that it has taken him upwards of one and half hours to pick up a newspaper because he has to stop and pass the time of day on the way with residents and fellow visitors that he has got to know! However, as we all know not everyone is looking for the same things in life. In contrast to Mark K, Sandra[10] stated the reason she kept returning to the "most beautiful island in the world" was that the local people bid her welcome but never imposed upon her! Clare[22] gave a personal example of how she thinks the views of the Island by residents and visitors might differ. While visiting Millport, she met her future husband who was brought up on the Island. Once they married and had set up home nearby on the mainland, she, and subsequently her children, have continued to visit at every opportunity and have a place on the Island. Her husband still talks of deprivations of growing up on a small island and is quite ambivalent about paying too many return visits! Josh[17] told a revealing tale of those relationships. When the bus arrived at the ferry terminal, the ferry was nowhere to be seen. His first inclination was to alight from the bus and wait for it outside, However, he was stopped by residents and visitors alike who basically said, stay with us in here and tell us a bit about yourself. He no longer felt a stranger.

Many visitors, including a couple of the participants, eventually have become permanent residents. This can be a retirement goal among the more senior, or a desire to find a way to fit into and contribute to the unique island community. Probably Eric's[3] intention was a combination of the two as he splits his time almost equally between homes in Millport and Gourock. Is there something that drives people to want to spend frequent and/or long periods of time on our little island? Mary[1] provided not one but two strong hints: Almost at the conclusion of the drive to Largs there is a gap in the wall fringing the road that allows a sudden dramatic vista of Great Cumbrae, which causes a fluttering in the heart and sometimes erratic driving! And the oft-mentioned joy of rounding Farland Point and sailing into Millport Bay. Unfortunately, unless there is some unanticipated change in ferry routes, that joy will be denied to future travellers to the Island. It can still, however, be experienced on a Waverley cruise and is highly recommended. A property which one can use as a base for further travel obviously appeals to some of the participants whose primary home is some distance from the Island. Again, I used to think that we were the only ones who had sussed out the value of having a base there and its proximity to Glasgow Airport and the M8 motorway to facilitate travel to Europe and to Scotland and the rest of the UK respectively. However, we are not alone as Mark K[20] noted. And of course, the accessibility of the Island appeals to just about every other lucky person to have a second home there. From virtually anywhere in central Scotland, one can suddenly get the urge in the morning to hop over to the other home and get some island air and be there in time for dinner (the vagaries of the ferries notwithstanding!) (Peter[12] and Eileen[13]).

One of the interesting perspectives that I gained from members of The Gallant Thirty Twa was from those whose relationship with the Island had been interrupted along the way. John[6] travelled specially to Millport to meet with me and was setting foot on the Island for the first time since 1976! His excuse for the absence---since the unfortunate incident when a window was broken in his rented digs and he was banned from returning, he had been unable to secure a satisfactory alternative and had instead travelled every year thereafter to Dunoon---I ask you! But don't let that make you think he was no longer a believer; I was overwhelmed (and I think maybe he was too) by his knowledge of the place and his desire to see things that he had not seen for a long time but still were fresh in his memory! Anne & Ian[9] were other victims of the difficulty in finding an accommodation vacancy after eight consecutive years of visiting. In their case, they had to decamp to Girvan for a while but fortunately they later found their way back and are now proud second homeowners and indeed my near neighbours.

We will now close this gentle investigation into "Why Millport?" with a look to the future, the inevitable future. A number of the participants are now of a mind that having managed to establish a strong relationship with the Island, they want it to be lasting; in fact, they want it to be everlasting. Without naming names, I can reveal that several plan to be buried or have their ashes scattered in some meaningful location. For one, that is not so surprising considering her grandfather and great-grandfather are already resting there. That seems to me the be the perfect post-script---I came for a weekend and stayed for an eternity!

Chapter 13

My Personal Thoughts x 32

XV The launches and boats at rest in Millport Bay.

The members of The Gallant Thirty Twa have done a sterling job in providing so much rich information on the topics I selected in advance. I trust I have been able faithfully to gather and report what was presented to me. Along the way, it seemed like each participant came up with at least one of what I would describe as a "nugget". A nugget was a quote or observation that was just too good to bury in the foregoing chapters. It deserved its own place in this chapter. Each is personal to the participant, but collectively they provide a fitting postscript to a piece of work that I hope the reader will enjoy and by the end will understand just what this amazing town on this amazing island is all about!

- "Messing around in rockpools searching out crabs and sea anemones was the ultimate pleasure for a child." (Mary[1])
- Millport was where this married couple first met so they do believe only good things happen there! (Seona & Gordon[5])
- And just to confirm it "I associate the Island with only good things." (Lorraine[2])
- "During Covid 19, the number of passengers was severely restricted on the ferry. I was the second person left in line when the CalMac employee made the cutoff. However, strangely enough, there were very few cars on this particular voyage. The only person in front of me thought he would try some science to get us onboard. He informed the employee that each car weighed about 4000 lbs and each passenger weighed about 150 lbs. So, he should be able to allow an extra 26 passengers to board for every car space that was unoccupied. That's interesting said the CalMac employee and walked on!" (The author snuck this one in!)
- Fond reminiscing about the round-island bus service that was present for a few years. At times it was a single decker, at others an open double decker. Perhaps its time has come again? (Wilson[8])
- "My mood always changes for the better when I step on to the ferry." (Suki[23])
- "Kids in Millport do not need iPads!" (Moira[28])
- When he was fishing on the west side of the Island----"It feels like you are on your own private island." (Kyle[24])
- "I still get into my Millport mood every June." (Bill[18])
- Heavy recollections of endless amounts of fun on the boats (for hire). (Mark K[20])
- "The only people not smiling were probably residents!" (Suki[23])

- "On wet days, the whole family of ten members would gather around the big oval table in the lounge and play the Newmarket card game with Swan Vesta matches to lay bets." (Fraser[32])
- Riding the Waverley is still on her bucket list of things to do. She had better not leave it too long! (Amanda[21])
- It was as much fun to visit the Island in the wilds of winter as it was in the heat (or wilds) of summer. (Mary[1])
- "If you go abroad for roughly the same cost as going to Millport, I suppose people will tend to go looking for the sun!" (Donald & Jennie[11])
- He recalled going tattie picking on the Island in August as a useful way of building up the holiday spending money. (Wilson[8])
- "It was essential for any house we were staying in to have jigsaws for the wet days." (John[6])
- The evening fishing parties were her favourite and she confessed to being a Mauchline fan. (Valerie[26])
- She recalled, with a hint of guilt, stealing apples from the gardens of the big houses on Marine Parade. (Eileen[13])
- Talking of guilt, he recalled teenage barbecues at Farland Point and trying to get high on Coca Cola and Aspirin! (Bill[18])
- By way of entertainment, she and her friends went round the caravan park after dark and threw pieces of bread on the roofs of the caravans. The early unscheduled morning wake-up calls were provided by the squawking seagulls! (Alison B[27])
- "Mother (Peggy Macrae) said I have seen the world, and there is no place like Millport." (Christine[30])
- The ultimate childhood escape was climbing the Lion Rock from tail to nose. (Fraser[32])
- "The horse droppings were quickly shovelled up by gardeners all over the Island." (Minia[31])
- "…with those summer friends, we were out to all hours, Millport was famously safe." (Christine[30])
- Joy was boating in Millport Bay, even if life jackets were not provided. (Liz[14])
- He has a particular fondness for the pictures of the old steamers hanging in Frasers Bar. (Josh[17])

- He recalled the days when all sorts of services like tonsils, appendixes, births, and emergencies were offered at the Lady Margaret Hospital. (Wilson[8])
- "My very first swimming lessons were in the harbour." (Seona & Gordon[5])
- "Peggy Macrae is unfairly overshadowed by her husband." A tribute to the great Island promoter. (Donald & Jennie[11])
- He misses and craves the ice cream with raspberry topping from the Ritz Café. (Josh[17])
- Her favourite beach was Kames Bay because it was sheltered, had clean sand, and toilets. Even the cold sea water was tolerable. (Mary[1])
- But! He recommended keeping your mouth closed when swimming near the town sewage pipe in Kames Bay! (Fraser[32])
- "Hunters was such a posh deli!" (Alison B[27])
- He so loved listening to the pipe band as it marched along the front, and when it was positioned on the pier for a visit of the Waverley. (Fraser[32])
- Heaven was a "chittery bite" after emerging from the cold sea. (Moira[28] and Christine[30])
- "Gran met Papa here in the 1920s and the family has been visiting ever since!" (Susan B[19])
- The Talisman was her all-time favourite steamer. (Moira[28])
- She recalled rowing out to the Eileans for picnics (and the unique view of the town) (Mary[1])
- He knew the almost secret way up from Marine Parade to the Farland Hills. The access is now effectively a total secret! (Wilson[8])
- Arriving on the Island must have felt the same as entering Narnia! (Amanda[21])
- "In the 1950s, there were more vehicles in a Glasgow car showroom window than on the whole of the Isle of Cumbrae!" (Bill[18])
- "I remember as a teenager wanting to spread my wings, thinking Millport was boring. I persuaded my family to try Lytham St Annes. What a disappointment. I never complained about Millport again!" (Eileen[13])

- Great reminiscing about the afternoon cruises on the Waverley, Duchess of Hamilton, and Duchess of Montrose. (Fraser[32])
- She lost a shoe in the boggy ground on the Farland Hill and later washed it off in the toilet bowl! (Evelyn[29])
- They commented on a rumour that the refurbishment of the Old Pier about 15 years ago directly contributed to the reason why the wooden section is now condemned today. (Seona & Gordon[5])
- "We loved the 10-month isolation during Covid. We experienced real island life!" (Spencer[16])
- "The best chippy in town was up a close and round the back where they cooked their chips on an open fire!" (Minia[31])
- Her late mother was an enthusiastic supporter of the Save the Waverley and Save the Pier movements. (Clare[22])
- "The old Fintry Bay Café was the best on the Island." (Moira[28])
- He loved playing the game of who would be first to see the funnel of the Talisman as it appeared from behind the rocks at Farland Point. (Fraser[32])
- "The weather (on the Island) always seemed better than it was in Largs!" (Christine[30])
- She fondly remembered the horses and donkeys on the beach. (Valerie[26])
- "We never attended services in the Cathedral because we were afraid it would eat into our holiday time!" (Seona & Gordon[5])
- "English people always seemed to fall in love with the place!" (Alison B[27])
- She related a sad story of visiting her brother who was suffering terribly from dementia and did not even recognize her. He was totally silent through a difficult visit until she brought out a book of old photographs and up he piped, "Oh, there's Millport!". (Name withheld)
- He recalled the adventure of hiring a motorboat and taking it over to Wee Cumbrae (against the rules), tying it up and going off to explore. On their return, they could not restart it and had to wait until much later to be rescued by the boat hirer. As they sheepishly reported in to their parents, they were informed that it had all been witnessed by them through binoculars from the Tavern bar! (Mark K[20])

- He remembered a man jumping off the rocks at Farland Point to swim with a basking shark. The man might have been off his rocks too! (Fraser[32])
- "No matter the tides and winds, the captain and crew of both the Ashton and Leven seemed undaunted, challenged even, by storms and in the worst weather their astonished passengers went up on deck, thrilled to approach the Millport Pier by sailing between the Eileans in the bay!" (Christine[30])
- However, sometimes the weather wins. She was boating when a storm suddenly sprung up and had to take refuge on the Eileans. She was stuck there until they could be rescued. (Valerie[26])
- She remembered when a drought hit the Island. Her job was to fetch drinking water from the Wishing Well and buckets of seawater to flush the toilet. (Mary[1])
- Our most senior participant at 95 years young contributed more than the average number of memories! (Author's observation)
- Only in Millport. She remarked that the unpaid labour in the stables and on the boats probably violated something. But the kids loved doing it. (Eileen[13])
- "The thing with holidaymakers was to go with your dad downstairs and join the spellbound huddle gazing at the mighty pistons (of the Talisman), an entire journey often spent watching the engines!" (Christine[30])
- They missed the big open launches operated by Hunter and Mauchline on the excursions in the afternoon and fishing parties in the evening. (Donald & Jennie[11])

Chapter 14

Afterthoughts

XVI Just how many children can say hello to the Crocodile Rock at one time?

Just like the children on the Croc Rock, we are teetering on the edge. The tale is almost done. It has been a huge pleasure for me. The participants were all fabulous. I knew some of them in advance but most I had never met before. They are now all friends! Whether we met in person or bumbled our way through the technology to converse in

Zoom or Messenger, the result always seemed to be the same----the participant would say "I don't know that I can be very much help to you. There is not really that much I can remember." They would then proceed to share more and more reminiscences as they came back into their minds! They confessed that some things they had not thought about for twenty, or forty, or even sixty years but back they came and crystal clear too. What could have been stilted one-way interviews almost invariably became two-way conversations. I learned a lot, when I had not necessarily expected to, and I shared a lot of things that were new to the some of the others. Some people came with sheets of notes--- they had obviously been giving the subject much thought in advance---and others came with nothing but tabula rasa. But the result seemed to be the same. A massive outpouring of memories, many a laugh, and just the right amount of sentimentality without it becoming mawkish!

What have I learned out of this interesting process? Those members of the Gallant Thirty Twa share a deep knowledge of a little town and the island it occupies. Though they came from completely different walks of life, they shared common knowledge, which was a bit of a surprise to me, and common values, which probably did not surprise me as I got to understand them. There is a real love for the place, and it came out unsolicited and volunteered. I could easily have attracted some or many who were negative about the place. In the end I did not encounter a single one. If I had broadened the project, would the outcomes have been the same? There is no way of knowing for sure, but I suspect that I could have doubled or even tripled the participation numbers and the results would have turned out roughly the same! It says a lot about Millport and the Isle of Cumbrae. Maybe it is cast in stone that only good things truly happen there.

As I look back, did I really have clear purposes for the project when I set out? One was of course to provide some entertainment for the reader. Or else, why do it! Now that it is being read, I would be fascinated to know if its impact is different for readers who were familiar with the subject matter as opposed to those who might never have heard of the place. Hopefully, that will emerge. Was there a desire to turn people on to my favourite place? Of course, there was. I take the greatest pride in making even the smallest contribution to the knowledge of the Island in the hope that readers will be stimulated to pay it a visit, for the first time in a long while or for the very first time. Hopefully, you now realize that a treat awaits you! And finally, there was a desire to make even a modest contribution to the wellbeing of an amazing community. Any island economy tends to remain forever tentative. More visitors, more part-time residents, and even more permanent residents, preferably with as many children as they can muster, can only enrich the community. They are its lifeblood.

Was there an intention to make the participants feel good about themselves? That sounds a little pretentious, but you know I have a hunch now that they all not only enjoyed the experience but also were very glad that they were in the position to share their happy memories. And for me, I can only say that it was a unique experience and yes, it does make me feel good!

What now? Is there a case for a book of permanent residents' memories? I suspect there most definitely is and as soon as possible. We have already lost some amazing historical resources on the Island and need to get things recorded for posterity before they disappear. It will probably not be me who takes the lead the next time but if someone else is stimulated after reading this book then a good job has been done,

In the meantime, don't forget to make your next trip, short or long, to you-know-where!

Hail to The Gallant Thirty Twa

I could not have done it without you all. Hope you had as much fun as I did!

1. Mary Bowman	Linwood, Renfrewshire, Scotland
2. Lorraine Rennie Giovanazzi	Wishaw, North Lanarkshire, Scotland
3. Eric Marshall	Gourock, Renfrewshire & Millport, North Ayrshire, Scotland
4. Susan McAtasnay	Paisley, Renfrewshire, Scotland
5. Seona & Gordon Black	Bonnybridge, Falkirk, Scotland
6. John Eastop	Glasgow, Scotland
7. Alison Rennie	Singapore
8. Wilson Black	Coatbridge, North Lanarkshire by way of Glasgow, Scotland
9. Anne & son Ian Coats	Motherwell, North Lanarkshire, Scotland
10. Dr Sandra McCallum	Troon, South Ayrshire, Scotland
11. Donald and mother Jennie Scobbie	Bonnybridge, Falkirk, Scotland
12. Peter McLean	Just beyond Caracas, Venezuela
13. Eileen Bandcroft	Auckland, New Zealand by way of Stranraer, Dumfries & Galloway, Scotland
14. Liz Stuart	Paisley, Renfrewshire, Scotland
15. Tracy McKernan	Inverkip, Renfrewshire, Scotland
16. Spencer Veitch	Glasgow, Scotland
17. Josh Roberts	Houston, Texas, USA
18. Bill Paterson	London, England by way of Denniston, Glasgow, Scotland
19. Susan Biggar	Beith, North Ayrshire, Scotland
20. Mark Kaltner	London, England & Millport, North Ayrshire, Scotland

21. Amanda Tennant	Motherwell, North Lanarkshire & Millport, North Ayrshire, Scotland
22. Clare Victoria McCulloch	Fairlie, North Ayrshire, Scotland
23. Suki McGregor	Glasgow and Largs, North Ayrshire, Scotland
24. Kyle Booth	Strathaven, South Lanarkshire, Scotland
25. Mark Cantle	Holtwhistle, Northumberland, England
26. Valerie Harvey	Cedar, British Columbia, Canada
27. Alison Brown	Broughty Ferry, Dundee, Scotland
28. Moira Wilson	Burnside, South Lanarkshire, Scotland
29. Evelyn McIntosh	Carluke, South Lanarkshire, Scotland
30. Christine Macrae	Glasgow, Scotland
31. Minia Miller	Glasgow, Scotland
32. Fraser Steel	Biggar, South Lanarkshire, Scotland

Acknowledgements

I would like to acknowledge and offer thanks to the following for use of their photographs that bring the words to life.

Number	Name	Page
Cover	Sonya Stuart	Cover
I	Sonya Stuart	Preliminary
II	Anon. via internet	Preliminary
III	Eric Marshall	1
IV	North Ayrshire Heritage Trails	7
V	Andy Muldoon	19
VI	paddlesteamers.org	28
VII	Anon. via internet	40
VIII	North Ayrshire Heritage Trails	49
IX	Scott Ferris	65
X	Sonya Stuart/Bronwyn Jenkins-Deas	74
XI	Anon. via internet	88
XII	Trip Advisor	98
XIII	Eric Marshall	107
XIV	Anon. via internet	119
XV	North Ayrshire Heritage Trust	127
XVI	Herald & Times Group	134

Errata

Before embarking on this project, I was telling a long-standing resident of the Island, who shall remain nameless, that I was going to focus on the views of visitors only and leave residents for some other project. He said I was wasting my time. "Visitors think they know all about Millport, but they don't. Only residents know." I beg to differ in the most vehement way on behalf of thirty-two friends!

But mistakes of memory are always possible and so I include this page for the future inclusion of any errors, should anyone wish to make me aware of them.

Printed in Great Britain
by Amazon